Dressage the
LIGHT WAY

Dressage the
LIGHT WAY

A CLASSICAL, NATURAL AND INTELLIGENT APPROACH TO TRAINING FOR *EVERY* HORSE AND RIDER

PERRY WOOD

J.A.ALLEN · LONDON

First published in Great Britain in 2012
J.A. Allen
Clerkenwell House
Clerkenwell Green
London EC1R 0HT
J.A. Allen is an imprint of Robert Hale Limited
www.allenbooks.co.uk

ISBN 978-1-908809-00-1

British Library Cataloguing in Publication Data
A catalogue record for this book is available from the British Library

Designed and typeset by Paul Saunders
Edited by Jane Lake
Photographs by Fiona Crawford except: Carl Hester images by Bob Atkins, courtesy
Horse & Rider Magazine; Paul Belasik images by Karl Leck, courtesy Paul Belasik;
Anja Beran images by Stefan Wartini and Stefanie Fuchs, courtesy Anja Beran.

Printed by Craft Print International Ltd, Singapore

Disclaimer of Liability

The author and publisher shall have neither liability nor responsibility to
any person or entity with respect to any loss or damage caused or alleged to
be caused directly or indirectly by the information contained in this book.
While the book is as accurate as the author can make it, there may be errors,
omissions, and inaccuracies.

Contents

Preface

The art of riding in its many forms is an expansive subject, not least because every horse and every rider is different and the possibilities and permutations are infinite. That doesn't mean there cannot be some guiding principles to act as signposts along the way, helping us to follow in the footsteps of other horsemen and benefitting from their knowledge, mistakes and discoveries. Ultimately though, each of us – you, me and anyone else who puts one leg either side of a horse's back – has to find their own way, their own experience and their own way of embodying the living art of riding. My aim in this book is to help you to find your own way, with the help of some guiding principles, values, exercises and ideas, many of which have been tried, tested and honed by years of dedicated practice with my own horses and by many, many students during my countless hours of teaching the subject around the world.

The horse is a noble, kindly and generous-spirited creature, and for that reason we surely owe it him to be the best we can be for him; this means constantly expanding our knowledge, being committed to improving our seat in the saddle and level of 'feel,' and being a calm and decent person for the horse to be around at all times. Good luck with your riding.

PERRY WOOD

Acknowledgements

It is a great privilege to have the opportunity to write this book for J. A. Allen and for that I am indebted to Lesley Gowers: I value her professionalism, insight, experience, sense of humour and friendship.

A very special thank you to the remarkable Anja Beran, Carl Hester and Paul Belasik for allowing me to feature photographs of their inspirational work in this book.

A big thank you to my fellow professionals who generously agreed to being quoted throughout the pages of the book and a posthumous 'thank you' to the late great masters whose words I have also quoted.

Thank you to the riders (students, friends and neighbours) and their wonderful horses who agreed to being photographed – in the middle of winter! – and appear in the pages of the book: Fiona Price-Jones and Relento; Emily Catford and Another Copper; Carly Willis and Murphy; Katherine McKenzie and CS Cotillion (Tilly); Caitlin Collins and New Mill Quarme; Jenny Watts and Ginger and Polly.

A warm-hearted thank you to all my students, you have no idea how much I learn from working with you and how much the learning process is a two-way street. I thank you for that two-way street, for your commitment to learning, for the effort of turning up with your nice clean horses – often having travelled a goodly distance – and for putting in the work between clinics/lessons. Thank you for our shared love and passion for horses and for the subject of fine riding, and for the friendship and mutual respect with which we interact.

A real horsey thank you to my horses, all of whom have taught me something. Some have taught me so much I cannot begin to measure, and some are still selflessly trying to teach me what they think I need to learn.

A big thank you to Fiona Crawford for her professionalism, great pictures and delightful manner in her role as photographer for the book.

I also wish to thank Samantha Elmhurst for her illustration of the dressage arena. Samantha J. Elmhurst BA Hons, artist and illustrator, www.livingart.org.uk

Finally, a respectful acknowledgement to you, the reader, for opening the pages of this book and seeking to expand or improve your horsemanship and riding for the mutual benefit of yourself and your horse: hats off to you.

Introduction

Anything forced cannot be beautiful...

– Xenophon

Would you like to dance with your horse? The answer to that question is usually a resounding 'Yes!' Whether you are a serious competitor, a rider who enjoys schooling their horse for pleasure or someone in between, you are almost certainly seeking the wonderful buzz of experiencing unity and harmony together with your horse in movement. That is what this book aims to do: to equip you with tips and training exercises to gymnasticise your horse, to show you ways to improve your riding and give you the keys to discovering new levels of connection and performance with your horse – all done with *lightness*.

Even if you don't want to 'do dressage,' you and your horse will benefit immensely from this type of training. In fact, whatever style of riding you enjoy, whether it is jumping, endurance, eventing, polo, trail riding or dressage you will have a lighter, safer, more athletic and responsive ride if you give your horse some good quality schooling as presented in this book.

The word 'dressage' conjures up all sorts of thoughts, responses and images for people, some good and some maybe not so good. Dressage does not necessarily mean performing a pre-prescribed sequence of movements in front of a judge. To my mind 'dressage' is a catch-all term for 'training on the flat' (i.e.

without jumps). So whenever you are developing the responsiveness, balance or gymnastic ability of a horse you could be said to be 'doing dressage'.

The derivation of 'dressage' is the French word *dresseur*, which means 'to dress' or 'to train'. The term has only been used to define competition riding since the very late 1800s. Since dressage means 'to train,' every time a rider sits on a horse they are 'doing dressage' whether they realise it or not, because every moment someone sits on a horse they *are* training him – either to go better or to go worse! The following sections will, therefore, let us set out to make sure it is always for the horse to go better.

A search for lightness

As we shall see, it is possible to go through the many stages of training the horse from basic schooling to High School/Grand Prix and find lightness.

Here are some of the things we are aiming for in *Dressage the Light Way*.

- The horse carries himself, which means he is truly in self-carriage and not needing to be pushed along with the rider's legs or held together with the rider's hands.

- The sensation is one of gracefulness and ease, both for the rider and for the horse (despite the horse offering maximum gymnastic effort).

- There is a sense of togetherness, connection, agreement, almost a secret alliance between the horse and rider.

- It seems as though the rider has a thought, a wish or an intention and the horse immediately performs whatever was in the rider's mind.

Riding with lightness is mostly a state of mind, adhering to values that support an empathic, artistic and natural union with the horse. It is a commitment to looking for the most effective, most subtle and gentle way to communicate your wishes to the horse and for him to respond with equal lightness in return, and you can do that from the first days of your ridden work together until the last.

Art or sport?

Training a horse can be viewed as an art, a sport or a bit of both. It depends on your approach and the aims and values behind your riding. If the primary goal is to win in competition then the work will have the flavour of a sporting endeavour. If you train your horse purely with the idea of creating a living example of beauty in movement then you will be heading into the territory of art.

Whether you want to make your training an art or a sport (or somewhere in between) you can do it without force by searching honestly for lightness in the way you and the horse communicate with one another.

What are the benefits of approaching dressage the *light way*?

1. The horse's working life is extended by helping him to use his muscles and frame in a beneficial manner.

2. The horse is more responsive to the rider's aids and requests.

3. The horse becomes more obedient, safer to ride and more relaxed in his attitude.

4. The horse looks more beautiful.

5. The horse feels more and more fantastic to sit on.

6. The horse improves and 're-finds' his natural balance and self-carriage under the weight of the rider.

7. The horse's suppleness, gaits and his way of going are developed.

> ≫ **When you see really great riding** and the horse going brilliantly you don't really see the rider doing anything. Is that because it looks great or because it works better? Both; but mainly because it works better.

History and Background

Far, far back in our dark soul the horse prances... The horse, the horse! The symbol of surging potency and power of movement...

– D. H. Lawrence

People have been riding horses for approximately six thousand years. The competition dressage sport we see today is a relatively new activity which only began around the beginning of the twentieth century. During those early decades it was almost exclusively the domain of the military. It was around this time that the FEI (Federation Equestre Internationale) was formed and set out its charter for the aims of the sport: it makes for interesting reading.

In previous centuries we can chart the progress of the dressage training of the horse in its classical guise through existing literature all the way back to the Greek general, Xenophon, some 2,500 years ago. The roots of dressage are to be found in the tradition of classical riding, which has been developed in various cultural centres around Europe, most especially since the Renaissance period, when the classical ideals of antiquity were revisited in all of the arts. Different European nations have developed the art of classical horse training in slightly different ways, which, quite understandably, reflect the personalities and lifestyles of the various regions. (The foundation for western riding also stems from classical riding, growing out of a style of riding taken to the Americas from Iberia in the early days of settlement in the New World).

For the majority of the millennia that man has been training horses to ride he has been doing so for the purposes of war, to hunt for food, as a means of transport or to work as a stock animal. It is not hard to imagine how important it would have been to have a well-trained horse for close combat in battle, since it could mean the difference between life and death for the rider. This would have been especially true for noblemen and royalty, whose lives would be of high value and who, therefore, would always need to be provided with brilliantly trained horses.

Classical riding is a term that is bandied about quite a lot these days, but what does the term 'classical' actually mean. Most people think of the word with reference to classical music. In music the 'classical' period was actually a very brief period which included Mozart, Haydn and early Beethoven. What characterised the music of that specific period was its order, clarity, lightness and balance of structure (the music of Mozart has especially well-ordered underlying structure). These principles had been taken up as a rebirth of the characteristics derived from the literary and artistic standards, principles and methods of the ancient Greeks and Romans. These are the pure methods and ideals adopted in the training of the classical horse of the period and which have survived and developed to this day. In modern parlance, if you say a pop song is a 'classic,' it means it has endured, been popular for more than a few weeks and has stood the test of time. Classical riding has done just that: stood the test of time, and the reason it has done so is quite simply because it works so well. But of course, just because something is simple doesn't mean it is easy!

>> **There have been a number** of important horsemen in the development of classical riding over the centuries – too many to discuss here. If you are interested in understanding more of the background to your horse training and its origins you may wish to look out works by Xenophon, De Pluvinel, De la Guérinière, Alois Podhajsky, Gustav Steinbrecht and Nuno Oliviera.

An engraving of horses training in the arena from the book by Antoine de Pluvinel, *Le Maneige Royal*, dated 1624.

Competition vs. Classical

The differences between competition dressage and classical riding are the subject of a great deal of discussion these days. Suffice to say that both are to some degree different and to some degree the same, but since their ultimate aim is quite different, the values, pressures and, therefore, methods of training may well vary.

The competition rider's aim needs to be to train a horse capable of winning the approval of the judges and of performing to the best of his ability on demand on the day of the competition in specific movements in a specific sequence in a specific time slot ... Now that is pressure!

The classical or natural rider who is principally producing a horse for the purposes of art or as a pleasure horse and partner has different aims: the rider and horse become an example of shared joy in each moment of their work together, and 'living art' is, in effect, the finished article during each of the horse's strides. They are theoretically under less restrictions and pressures of time and therefore able to approach the work with a different mind-set from the competition trainer. Of course a classical or a natural trainer may have other pressures and high ideals: their own sense of expectation; a wish to work at the uppermost level of their art; the wish to maintain the lightness in the work; and a wish to maintain their connection and sense of shared joy with the horse through sharing their movement.

Natural riding

The term 'natural' usually refers to working with empathy and understanding of the true nature of the horse. It means to understand the natural psychology of the horse and to work with him in that knowledge, rather than treating him as a furry machine upon which we force our demands.

The benefits of embracing the horse's nature in our riding are numerous:

- he becomes a more willing partner, offering up his own energy and ideas

- he is generally more relaxed in different environments

- there is a higher degree of trust between horse and rider

- the horse offers less resistance

- he is safer to be around

- horse and rider create a more fun/joyful attitude together.

> >> **According to the dictionary,** 'natural' means formed by nature or instincts.

How can dressage be natural?!

Of course it is not natural for a human to sit on a horse at all. Nor is it natural for us to keep horses in stables or even in a limited area such as a paddock. You could argue that anything we do with prey animals such as horses other than hunting them for food is unnatural. So how can we integrate the ideal of being 'natural' with our horses into our riding and training?

One of the most important foundations for dressage, classical riding and any other valid form of training is that it is based upon the *natural* movements of the horse. Let me spell that out: dressage should work *with* the nature of the horse's gaits, which means it should be as 'natural' as possible! Not only should the movements be natural for the noble animal, it is also important that the progressive training of the horse is carried out with empathy and understanding for the nature of his mind, instincts and ways of being, as well as for his body and the way he moves.

Much of today's wave of 'natural riding' has grown out of the tradition of western riding, where the 'finished' horse is ultimately ridden on a totally loose contact, but that doesn't mean that the correctly-trained western horse doesn't work with his back well-rounded and his hindquarters engaged forwards under his body, helping him to be stronger in his back and facilitating the muscular development for him to carry the weight of a rider.

Riding on a loose rein with the horse relaxed through his frame may not cause problems, but to help the horse to adjust to the unnatural requirements of carrying a human on his back (something evolution has not yet designed the horse's back to do) it can help the horse's physical wellbeing to be ridden and trained to collect himself and round his back under the rider. Without rounding the horse's back at least enough of the time to strengthen him, too much downward pressure from the rider's body into the animal's back can cause physical weaknesses to develop into discomfort or soundness problems, which may then also appear to the rider as behavioural issues, contact problems and general unhappiness about being ridden.

> **》 It is interesting to note that** most apparently behavioural, attitude or emotional issues in the horse are actually manifestations of underlying physical discomfort or pain – real or remembered.

The challenge for every rider is to acquire enough knowledge, feel and skill that they can help the horse to work into a beneficial shape with lightness and finesse, thus helping him to readjust his balance under the weight of the rider so that not too much of the emphasis is on his front legs; this is one of the things that defines the true art of riding.

Basically, if you really care about the horse, long-term, he needs you to help him to be strong enough to carry you off into the sunset. The information in this book is designed to help you to achieve that result.

>> **It is important to be aware** that strengthening and suppling the horse is an on-going, never-ending project, but one which will bring endless rewards to anyone who dedicates themselves to riding with the horse's wellbeing in mind.

Keys to Using this Book

The information in this book is explained in the simplest way I can and technical terms for particular movements and exercises that you may or may not be familiar with are defined in each section, particularly those terms that are not immediately self-explanatory, such as travers and renvers. At the back of the book there is a diagram of the usual layout of the riding arena and where the arena letters are positioned. Using these letters gives us a universal language with which to structure what we are doing with the horse and helps us to have a plan and to know whether we are succeeding in riding accurately or just doodling about.

Much of this book talks about principles, values and having the right approach, but there is also a great deal of practical 'how-to' information too. However, just doing the 'how-tos' without the right principles and values behind our work with horses generally fails to produce the same quality of results, both for us and especially for the horses we ride.

This book is made up of lots of short sections, each addressing a small part of the subject of training your horse. Although they are presented in some kind of sequential order, it by no means implies you should stick to the order of the sections when training your horse; every horse is different, and through the course of training we sometimes have to backtrack (or even branch out sideways) to find a solution.

During all of our work it is worth bearing in mind a few of these points about the horse's nature.

- Horses are prey animals, which means practically all behaviours and responses they show are the result of being afraid of being eaten.

- Horses have a limited attention span. They also need variety and stimulation in order to maintain their attention for longer.

- Horses in general are not stubborn animals but are actually quite compliant. When they appear stubborn or resistant it is usually because they don't understand or find the request too difficult.

- Horses respond very well to positive reinforcement, being left in peace and comfort rather than negative reinforcement or punishment. Unfortunately, due to their prey animal nature, they usually view punishment as confirmation that they were right to be afraid of you!

- When the horse feels safe and trusts the rider he is massively more likely to stretch out of his limitations and will do far more than if he lacks trust or feels unsafe.

- Horses like to please and like to have a quiet life.

- Horses like to have fun.

- Horses are creatures of habit. You can use this to your advantage during training. You can also allow it to work against you if you are not careful!

- Horses will generally choose the easiest option: all you have to do is make the thing you want them to do look like the easiest option and you're home and dry.

- Horses have amazing memories, especially for emotionally charged experiences.

Riding by Magic – the Essence of Lightness

...Descente de main et descente de jambe...
(relax the hands and relax the legs)
– De la Guérinière (eighteenth-century riding Master)

Relax the aids whenever you can

When the horse is doing what you're asking you can cease giving active aids. If you continue to give aids when he is already doing the work, you will dull him and blunt the effectiveness of your aids; you may also inadvertently interfere with the flow of the horse's movement. So, whenever the horse is doing what you want, relax the aids and just sit there looking good for as long as possible!

'Model' the softness

Your horse can only be as magnificent as you are and he can only be as light or balanced as you are, so you have to 'model' the way you want the horse to be. That means making sure you are not unintentionally tight or blocked anywhere in your body, seat, legs, arms or hands, because the horse will inevitably reflect it in his way of going. Make sure you are free from blocks or tightness throughout, unless you are using a specific, localised increase of muscle-tone for a particular reason (see 'Bracing the back', overleaf).

Dressage champion Carl Hester in a beautiful half-pass.

'Bracing your back' and not 'bracing your back'

The concept of 'bracing the back' is something which some riders use to collect or half-halt the horse. It is an internal change in the use of the spine of the rider, and is best practised as a momentary increase in tone or tension in the back. Of course to do that you first have to be able to ride with your back not braced, which means supple and free (otherwise it will be braced all the time). The back being braced too much of the time can easily be the result of trying too hard, being told to 'sit up' a lot, or thinking you have to sit too tall on the horse without knowing how to stay released down into the saddle.

Precede every action with the idea of lightness

Before every action have the idea of being the softest or lightest you can be; that means starting every aid like a whisper, even if you don't think the horse is responsive, for if you always start your communications lighter than you think necessary, the horse will become more responsive. So before each action or aid, imagine the lightest you can possibly be, wait a moment and see what happens.

If you want to achieve true lightness it is important to maintain a constant awareness of the nature of the communication between yourself and the horse, which means: *feeling* the lightness and quality of the rein contact in both reins; *feeling* the nature of contact and responsiveness between your legs and the sides of the horse; and being aware of the gentle connection and interactions happening between your seat and the horse's body, and between his back and your back.

Yield the reins whenever possible

Sometimes you can put some lightness into your work by yielding or simply relaxing the reins within the contact. That doesn't mean throwing the contact away or suddenly dropping the connection, as this could well flop the horse onto his forehand, but it does mean feeling for the times when you can yield somewhat, give the horse the opportunity to stay in self-carriage without a direct contact, and allow him more space to flow and express himself in his work. Something else which can be explored with great effect is to yield the inside rein if the horse already has a good bend to the inside. For example if you are making a small circle or shoulder-in, try moving your inside hand forwards a little, trusting him to maintain the bend and giving him more space in which to move; you will probably be surprised at how nicely he goes.

Supple, supple, supple

Help the horse to become supple throughout his body, from his nose to his tail; a really supple horse will be a priceless, willing partner for you. The exercises in this book will give you the tools you need to create and maintain a beautifully supple and obedient companion, capable of more than you might imagine – supple, supple, supple.

Riding should not be a work-out for the rider

If riding your horse is like a work-out in the gym you are doing something wrong. If either one of you should be doing the hard work it ought to be the horse, whilst you are the mind behind the performance, the one who is directing things intimately through to the horse from your centred position up there in the saddle. If you are working really hard, stop and think really hard instead: ask yourself what you want and what can you do differently in order to achieve it.

Ride by magic

By 'riding by magic' I mean attempting particular movements, turns or transitions without consciously giving any physical aids. Children seem to be able to believe in this way of riding more easily than adults!

The art of riding is far more subtle than simply 'doing stuff' to make the horse perform. There are always further untapped layers of refinement and secret nuances between horse and rider to be discovered. Ultimately riding becomes a series of quiet thoughts in the mind of the rider, which the attuned equine partner 'hears' and acts upon with willing grace. How does one go about creating such experiences on a regular basis? By setting out to do as little as possible by way of physical actions and by being totally clear about your intentions. The more we set out to ride with just the mind and with no discernable physical aids – by magic – and to trust the horse to give us what we are asking for, the more possible it becomes to fine-tune the mystical connection and physical performance between horse and rider.

> **» Riding by magic not only gives** both horse and rider an experience of subtle connection, it also enables the horse to flow and express more freely in his movement, because the rider is not 'cluttering' the space or interfering with the horse's natural abilities by giving too many physical instructions.

The Seat and Position

...Down from the waist they are Centaurs

– William Shakespeare

The rider's seat and position are key ingredients in helping the horse to produce great results. Although there are some underlying ideals and principles that we want to follow, there is no single correct riding seat and position. The simple fact is that every rider's body is a different shape, every horse is a different shape and the cut of the saddle has a contribution to make too. The seat is a tool for communicating and assisting the horse, which means you may sometimes have to change it from one move to the next in order to attain the best results.

> ≫ **Horses are moment-to-moment** feedback machines, which means that, in order to know how one should sit, all we have to do is look at how the horse is working. Every adjustment to your seat or position that is right for that horse at that time will result in an instant improvement in his way of going and his responses to the aids.

How to develop a good seat and position

- Ideally the rider sits in a poised but relaxed position, allowing the seat to fully 'be' on the saddle. Not squeezed up above it by sitting up too tall, or slumped by sitting too crumpled.

- Allow the upper arms to hang relaxed by your sides. Allow your legs to hang as freely as possible down the horse's sides.

- The seat needs to move totally *with* the horse's back, which means it has to be free, mobile and under the rider's control.

- It is a mistake to simply let the horse move your seat - you would instantly be left behind the movement and become an encumbrance to the poor horse. It is also a mistake to push with the seat too hard, as that makes his back uncomfortable and your back stiff. A happy medium between being passive and active with the seat should give the rider the unity with the horse's movement which is needed.

- Sit well into the front of the saddle, with your feet below and in line with your seat, and your shoulders above your hips.

- It is generally a mistake to tip backwards behind the vertical with the upper body, although it is almost universally practised and many teachers instruct students to do it. Sitting behind the vertical puts you behind the movement; it makes some horses dip their backs and hollow, some horses rush away and many just get lazy or heavy because they are waiting for the rider at every step. Contrary to what you may think, tipping back does not help the horse to put more weight on his hindquarters.

- 'Thinking' forwards and up with the top of the head will have a good effect on lengthening the rider's spine without making it stiff.

- Try just 'thinking' of opening the sternum (chest).

- Relax the back of your waist frequently.

- Use a saddle that works for you and the horse. If one of you is struggling with the saddle (or the position in which it places you), change it.

Fiona is sitting with poise and balance; her upper arms are hanging downwards and her head is placed nicely over her shoulders. She is using body tone within her aligned position to collect the horse for maximum expression in his trot.

- Experiment with different angles of your upper body: roll forwards a little, roll back a little. Which way helps the horse? He will tell you immediately.

- Experiment with minute adjustments to the angle of your seat: tuck it a little further under you, release your core downwards, bring your core up. Put more tone into your stomach muscles, or release the stomach. Which way helps the horse? He will tell you immediately.

- Try subtly different variations of the ways to sit in the different gaits. The horse will show you what works by moving more smoothly, more rhythmically or by going rounder (more on the bit) with lightness.

- The human head is heavy and needs to be in the best position to help the horse stay light. Try looking in different places with just your eyes and then by moving your whole head and see how it influences the horse. As a rule the rider is best looking above the horse's ears, in the same direction as the horse all the time; slight variations during different movements may help.

The Right Mental Attitude

Learning is movement from moment to moment

– J. Krishnamurti

The mental attitude of the rider is of paramount importance. Basically, if you can't get into the right emotional and mental state it may be best not to ride and, instead, leave it for another day. Horses are incredibly sensitive creatures and so if you are not in the right zone inside, the horse will pick up on it and feed it back to you by becoming tense, resistant or even afraid of his own shadow.

What is the right mental attitude?

Non-judgment

Being judgmental is a cultural habit in all aspects of our lives, so it is no wonder that judgment rears its head when we ride horses and all our insecurities can come bubbling to the surface. Try to become aware of the internal judgments you make about yourself or your horse or the way things are going when you ride. Being judgmental makes you feel bad, and when you

>> **Why is the right mental attitude** so important? Because the rider's mind influences the rider's body and the rider's body influences the way the horse uses his body.

feel bad you ride worse, and when you ride worse the horse goes worse; it's a no-brainer!

Drop all forms of judgment when you ride and just feel each moment with your horse one after the other.

Calm

It is important to be calm on the inside so that you can be calm on the outside. With calmness your thinking is clearer and you will be better able to make the right moment to moment decisions whilst riding. Also, when you are calm your body language, seat and aids will all be more centred, refined and clearer. A calm rider is not in a fearful state; we have all heard it said that horses can smell fear – and they can!

Patient

Horses can drive you crazy if you let them. It takes a lot of time and patience to train a horse. Without endless patience it is easy to become frustrated and tense, which causes the quality of the riding and communication to deteriorate.

Loving

Unless we are consistently loving to the horse, not just when grooming or petting him in the stable but during every moment of the ride, the chances are he will feel the need to defend himself on some level or other. When we are loving towards the horse we ride with a gentler feel, it helps him to feel safe and willing to work with us in the deepest sense, and protects us and the horse from the risk of the work deteriorating into forceful, aggressive or even abusive training.

Present

Horses live totally in the moment, which means that if we want to create true connection with the horse we must join him in the present moment. Being very present is a deeply rewarding state to be in anyway, and one of the reasons why riding can be such an addictive and relaxing antidote to the rest of our busy lives. Many people liken their best experiences of riding to being like a meditation, where time stands still and they lose themselves in the divine moments with the horse. It is possible to develop the practice of being present: you could say it is essential if you want to have consistently rewarding experiences with horses.

Detached

Staying emotionally detached whilst riding is a massive boon. Becoming emotionally entangled in the work, whether by getting into a negative spiral, becoming too determined or getting overly ambitious can seriously interfere with the way the horse goes. Many people ride because they want it to make them feel good, which is fine on one level; the problems arise when it doesn't go to plan (for whatever reason) and then the rider fails to get the good feeling they want from the ride. It is best to go to the horse each day with an open, detached heart and mind and see where it takes you, rather than trying to recapture a feeling that existed on a previous day.

Focussed

Because horses are prey animals, it is useful to have a peripheral awareness of everything going on around you whilst you ride, so you have some idea of what may or may not affect the horse's behaviour. At the same time, try to keep your mind focussed on what you are doing. If you are riding and at the same time thinking about what to cook for dinner, what someone at work said to you or what the people leaning on the arena fence might think about your riding, then you are not focussed enough. When you are on a horse you need to be fully with him in your mind, feeling every single thing that is going on in one moment after another and working with him to make each part of the dance happen beautifully.

Respectful

Horses are extraordinarily noble creatures, simultaneously capable of incredible power, sensitivity and gentleness. It is important to respect the qualities the horse willingly gives to us. It is also important to respect the nature of the horse, his needs, instincts and innate fears. It is wise to respect the horse for his physical strength and ability to cause mayhem and serious injury as a result of that physical strength, his fears, and speed. In some situations it is easy to forget that the horse is a living, feeling, breathing creature with his own thoughts, desires and ideas and not just a vehicle for our own ambitions or fascinations. Without respect for the soul of the horse, true connection is lost and the concept of riding as an art loses its deeper value.

Positive

Carly enjoying a positive and fun attitude to the work with her four-year-old Irish horse, Murphy.

For the horse to enjoy being ridden and enjoy the company of someone, that someone needs to be pleasant and positive to be around. If everything the horse tries is met with disapproval or a blank expression, pretty soon he will

stop bothering. If, however, the rider is positive and encouraging, the horse will invest more and more of himself in working with the rider to find solutions and right answers. He will also like to spend time with the rider and work with more joy and expression in his steps.

Trusting

It is important to trust the process of training and allow it to unfold in a natural way, rather than trying to push things along too quickly and resort to force. It is important to trust yourself – your balance, your ability and your seat. Finally it helps to trust the horse (not in an unrealistic sense); if you trust the horse to play his part, you are more likely to be relaxed in the saddle, which will help everything go more swimmingly.

Getting in the Zone

There is something about the outside of a horse that
is good for the inside of a man.

– Sir Winston Churchill

We have looked at how important it is to have the right attitude when you ride, but not everyone is adept at getting in the zone reliably every time they ride, so here are some ideas on how to do just that.

- From your first moments on the horse do a quick scan of where he is at: feel how he responds to each of your legs separately, feel how he responds to each of the reins individually, feel how he responds to your seat and balance when you slow down, or free up, or 'collect' yourself.

- Make a decision to be an objective observer of your riding and of the horse whilst you ride.

- Don't take it personally if things don't go to plan, or if you fail to get what you got yesterday or last week or even last year. Avoid thinking 'the horse is playing me up'.

- Feel inside your own body, raise your body-awareness; check where you can release yourself, where you might be holding tension or where you may be blocking the flow of the movement.

- Do something simple that you are confident doing and that you know settles the horse into the work space too.

- Picture your energy dropping down through your body, through your seat and down into your feet so you are well grounded.

- Away from the horse you can explore how to access the zone by such practices as meditation or the Alexander Technique. These practices teach you to bring your awareness and your mind under your control more readily so that when you ride you have another way of accessing the right type of state.

A sense of calm concentration and a lovely connection between horse and rider pervades this picture of Caitlin and four-year-old Warmblood mare Quarme.

Leading classical rider Paul Belasik has been very eloquent in his exploration of riding as a meditation. Here he demonstrates how horse and rider are connected, listening to one another and in the zone whilst performing the piaffe.

- Focus 100 per cent of your attention on keeping the horse's attention (see The Attentive Horse, for how to do that).

- Make your body language support the kind of state you want to be in; for example, if you want to feel confident and calm, breathe well into your stomach in slow breaths, sit with your head up and legs and arms relaxed. Your body will then inform your brain that you are feeling more confident and calm.

Trust, Friendship and Connection

Personally I would rather have my horse see me as more of a partner than a dictator. More like, 'Let's do this together.'
– Mark Rashid

For me, unless the horse and I enjoy our time and our work together it is void of joy. So above all else what we are aiming to achieve, maintain and enjoy is a sense of connection with this magnificent creature.

To be trustworthy requires us to be our best selves at all times around the horse, to be aware of any negative emotions such as fear, anger or frustration when they are but a tiny seed inside us, so they do not sour our interaction with the horse and give him reason not to trust us. It is important to be absolutely consistent, so the horse becomes secure in the knowledge that he can trust us; for example, if one day we allow him to nibble us in a 'friendly' way and the next day whack him for biting he's probably not going to be too trusting anymore.

To me, connection with the horse means having a genuine love for the animal and sensing some indication from him that the feeling is mutual. Horses build quite solid connections with one another in the herd, so it is programmed into the horses DNA to be able to form close bonds. What we have to do is figure out how to create the desire in him to bond with us.

Kate and her Arabian mare Tilly enjoying a few moments of friendship and connection.

How to develop connection

- Physical touch, stroking the horse (not just conciliatory patting) can help him to relax and trust us.

- Be considerate of his likes and dislikes.

- Cause him no pain, discomfort or harm (and remember horses are *very* sensitive to physical discomfort and pain, and have fantastic memories).

- Work with him in ways that are consistent with the highest ideals of horsemanship.

- Do not think you have to *dominate* him or 'sort out' his emotional issues – they are quite likely just your own interpretation of something that may or may not be happening for the horse.

- Work within a comfort zone for you and the horse and gradually expand it; that way you can both maintain a sense of security and sanity together which will ultimately build into mutual courage and trust.

- Never take too much from the horse or push him too hard. This is especially important with school work, and the more advanced the work, the more demanding it is upon the horse anyway. It can be easy to mistakenly take too much from a sluggish horse (who may have good reason for being sluggish) or a fizzy over-forward horse (who is running on adrenaline and won't thank you for working his legs off).

- Use your intelligence and awareness to work and progress the horse as much as possible, rather than throwing endless amounts of equestrian knowledge (or nonsense) at the wall and hoping some sticks! Spend quality time with the horse *not* working him, just being, hanging out and standing with him, admiring him, etc.

- Take good care of all of his physical, emotional and mental needs.

- Be a good friend.

The Calm Horse

...when riding is used as an art form, as a meditation, it is one of the greatest and most revolutionary relationships between species...
– Paul Belasik

It is difficult for the horse to concentrate or be in a receptive learning state if he is not calm in his mind and body. Horses are quite good at being over-excited, fearful or tense. Unfortunately, any of these emotional states are counter-productive when it comes to wanting to achieve good work with the horse. When he is emotionally tense he will carry that tension in his muscles too, which means we cannot achieve the level of relaxation or connection we seek.

How to create a calm horse

- Make your aids quiet, consistent and smooth.

- Sit in a relaxed way, exude calmness, but remain alert and present.

- If the horse is too tense to ride, take some time on the ground leading him around the work area, or do some of the groundwork and in-hand exercises described in this book.

- Rub the horse slowly with the flat of your hand in places he likes (neck and shoulder are usually good to start with).

- Stand beside him and try stroking slowly and gently down his legs and hooves to the ground with a long riding stick until he relaxes.

- Use open relaxed reins to invite him to turn this way and that in walk. Guide him in the directions you ask for, but be flexible; you can always make things more accurate once the horse is settled in his mind.

- Hold and support him *gently* with your legs and reins, like holding a newborn baby.

- Postpone any predetermined goals or plans you may have had for the riding session; instead work with what you think he can easily cope with in a step-by-step way.

- Ride circles and turns rather than straight lines, stay away from the edges of the arena or an area where he may be more afraid or tense, i.e. stay in his comfort zone and allow the comfort zone to expand gradually on its own.

A calm horse and rider enjoy their morning work together: the author with semi-retired mare Fantastique, nineteen years old (the horse, not the author!)

The Attentive Horse

If one can only see the world through one's own eyes and is incapable of appreciating that it is perceived very differently through the eyes of the horse, one will inevitably be surprised by various of the latter's actions...

– Kurt Albrecht (director Spanish Riding School in Vienna 1974–1985)

You could be the world's greatest rider, but if the horse isn't listening to you, you won't get very far at all. The importance of having the horse's attention is often underestimated and is something worth addressing above everything else.

> **» Nothing works very well without** having the horse's full attention... When the rider assumes responsibility for being the leader the horse feels safe and can relax.

The reasons for horses being inattentive are perfectly natural: horses are interested in their surroundings, because their survival as a prey animal depends on knowing what dangers may be around the next corner. Also, being sociable

The horse's ears are a great indicator of where his attention is being directed; if they are focussed on the rider, that's a good sign.

herd animals, horses are naturally keen to focus on other horses rather than focus on their rider.

Horses don't really *want* to focus on the environment in preference to focussing their attention on their rider, they would far sooner the rider be the leader and take responsibility for the safety of the horse and themselves. But if the rider is not up to the job of being the leader, the horse will find himself with no option but to take responsibility, be alert to the surroundings and therefore not pay attention to the rider.

> ≫ **The nice thing about an attentive horse** is that he will relax, the aids can become lighter and he shies and spooks less.

How to get the horse's attention

- Ask the horse to look to the inside of the arena or bend his head in the direction of travel using a simple request with the inside rein (use a slightly open rein, i.e. an inch or two away from the horse's neck). As soon as the horse responds by following a feel on the rein, relax the aid. Repeat as many times as necessary. Do this whether you are riding or leading from the ground.

- If the request to bend to the inside doesn't work or he won't follow the feel of your direct rein aid to look away from whatever he is distracted by, make a small circle (6m or 8m in walk, slightly larger in trot) in the *opposite* direction to the source of his interest. This will inevitably lead him to bend in your desired direction. Repeat as necessary. It is much better to be intelligent than to fight about where he is looking.

- Shift the horse's focus by finding something absorbing and interesting for him to do, e.g. constant changes of direction or transitions up and down.

- Work in an area of the arena where he feels safer and is less distracted. It pays to work within the horse's comfort zone, improve the quality of the conversation between you, increase his relaxation and his responses to the aids and then expand the working area to include more 'distracting' areas.

- Stay incredibly attuned to your horse and keep his focus with you *before* it goes; that means noticing the very moment his mind begins to wander, rather than waiting until his focus has gone altogether.

- Get in the habit of asking for the horse's attention all the time whilst leading him, that way he will find it easier to understand the rules: when you're around he has to stay attentive to you.

- When riding, feel the relaxation of the bit in his jaw as he carries it contentedly and attentively. When his mind starts to wander, the first thing you may feel is one side of his jaw becoming a little tighter on the bit. A gentle and momentary play with the fingers inside the contact on the tightened side can help keep him in a state of relaxed attention.

- Likewise, you may feel the horse go a little solid against your leg on one side as his attention starts to wander (usually the opposite side to the direction in which he is planning to gaze at the horizon), so a *gentle* reminder with that leg or a *light* little touch of the stick can bring his attention back to you and away from the distraction.

Gymnastics and Yoga for Horses

...If a horse is not entirely free and supple, it cannot obey the will of the rider with ease and grace ... suppleness necessarily produces docility, because the horse then has no difficulty in executing what is commanded...

– François Robichon de La Guérinière

Much of this book is about gymnastic and yoga training for horses. This type of work can benefit horse and rider in a whole range of ways. One of the major benefits is that it helps the horse to become more flexible, supple and internally stronger. For many riders it is hard to imagine just how consistently amazing a horse can be to ride if you help him to be supple and balanced and to maintain that level of suppleness and balance. Every minute you spend working with your horse in this way will reward you amply in the long run.

I use the term 'yoga' because much of the work we can undertake to help the horse is of a stretching and suppling nature and can be carried out quite steadily and thoughtfully on the part of horse and rider. Not all of the work required needs to be carried out at a blustery working trot where we rush around the arena.

Because the right gymnastic and yoga training for the horse helps to make things easier for him physically, he naturally becomes more obedient and more ready to say 'yes' to the rider's requests.

Riders are often surprised to hear that apparent behavioural issues, diso-bedience or resistances from the horse are actually expressions of physical limitation; the horse is simply finding it too difficult or uncomfortable to respond with ease to the rider's requests because his body has not been adequately developed. With the right progressive training (i.e. gymnastics and yoga for the horse), the rider should experience more and more compliance from the horse, simply because the horse has become physically capable of responding and no longer needs to resist.

> **It is important to understand** that the job of suppling the horse is on-going: it requires regular training in the same way as a human dancer or athlete would need to keep up with their training. It is a job for life – *in a good way.*

So, how do we set about helping the horse to become flexible, supple and strong? To put it simply, we need to supple three major sections of the horse: the front end – the jaw, poll and neck; the hindquarters – the hips, hocks and fetlocks; and his middle – the ribs, stomach muscles and back.

Another way to look at the job of suppling is that we need to supple the horse laterally, which means he is good at bending and yielding side to side throughout his length; and we need to supple him longitudinally, which means he is good at flexing and rounding himself over his topline (his back and neck) and shortening or lengthening his spine from croup to poll.

There are a variety of tools that can help to improve the horse's supple-ness, including transitions, lateral work, carriage and impulsion. The way we choose which exercise to do at any given time or the way we juxtapose different exercises will help the horse to improve in different ways.

Programme of gymnastics and yoga

1. Lungeing and in-hand work form a good starting point from which to work with your horse's physical ability.

2. Flexions of the jaw, neck and poll in hand (and later from the saddle) can also help many horses to find lightness and understanding of the aids.

3. Ride some circles smaller than 20m (e.g. 6m in walk and 8m or 10m in walk and trot).

4. Ride a great many transitions, ideally with invisible aids and with the horse remaining in the same shape/carriage through the transitions. It can help to do these on 20m circles, since the arc of the circle will help to keep the horse more rounded and on the aids.

5. Practise shoulder-in daily from the saddle (walk and trot), and in hand (in walk).

Shoulder-in

A famous picture of the shoulder-in from the book School of Horsemanship by François Robichon de la Guérnière, first published in 1729.

6. Introduce travers (haunches-in), renvers (haunches-out) and half-pass in walk, trot and eventually in canter.

7. Piaffe and passage can add the finishing touches to the gymnastic training of the horse.

Lateral movements (here a shoulder-in performed in hand) done regularly and with care are a superb way to help the horse become flexible, supple and strong.

Yoga work in walk

If you travel around watching people work their horses in arenas, mostly you see the work being done in trot. Trot is the best overall gait because it has forwardness and is a symmetrical gait – the horse moves in equal diagonal pairs of limbs. Far less work is generally seen in canter and not a great deal is seen in walk. There are disadvantages to working in walk, in that the impulsion of the horse may be lost and, if the work is not kept interesting enough, the horse may fall asleep with his eyes open! However, there is a great deal of value to be gained from work in a collected, steady walk with the horse nicely on the aids, not least because both horse and rider have time in the walk to figure out what they are doing or supposed to be doing, without the added speed, forward momentum and bounciness of the trot.

A request for a gentle piaffe in-hand can help gymnasticise the more advanced horse, even into older age.

Ideas for beginning work in walk

- Walk on the outside track of the arena and make a snake-like pattern when you alternately guide the horse in off the track by a couple of metres, and then back to the track – all with the minimum rein aids.

- Begin with a large circle, and then at certain points on the 20m circle, e.g. each time you cross the centre line or reach the fence, ride a 6m circle.

- Ride a 6m circle on each school letter, go straight in between the letters, but maintain a steady pace and collection

- Ride a 6m circle at every school letter and shoulder-in along the track in between each of your circles.

- Ride walk–halt transitions, making a halt specifically after every six or eight strides of walk.

- Alongside the fence, make a few steps of rein-back with a light feel in the reins every 20 or so strides of walk.

- Ride shoulder-in on a big circle (15m or 20m), and then intersperse the occasional tiny circle (4m or 6m) in shoulder-in.

- From shoulder-in on the 20m circle go into travers for say ten or fifteen steps, then back to shoulder-in again.

- Ride half-pass from the corner of the arena to the centre (letter X), make a half pirouette in walk and half-pass back to the corner you started from.

- Ride half-pass (or leg-yield if the horse is not ready for half-pass) from the centre line at letter A or C to the fence, and at the fence ask the horse to go along the track bent to the outside of the arena in a counter shoulder-in.

> **>> The shoulder-in is perhaps the single** most effective means of developing the horse's strength and suppleness. A horse who is well-versed in shoulder-in at the walk and trot and who is asked to perform the movement regularly in both directions will almost inevitably improve his way of going, his responsiveness to the rider and his overall performance. (See The Shoulder-in)

In-hand Work 1

Work in hand helps the horse to gain trust and confidence...
it also makes it possible to collect the horse well without the
rider's weight...

– Richard Hinrichs

The in-hand work explored in this section is intended to begin a conversation which helps to create a classically light, collected and naturally responsive riding horse. For the purposes of this book I shall assume the horse has already been well-handled, backed and is already going under saddle.

The question of whether you work the horse with a bit or bitless is entirely personal. It is important to understand, though, that by the very nature of how different bridling arrangements work, from the standpoint of biomechanics, they will have different effects on the way the horse responds and the results created. I will assume at this stage that the horse will be working in a simple jointed snaffle bit, as this is the most common arrangement for the early part of the horse's training.

You need to be clear what your aims are with working in hand: you want to teach the horse to understand the aids in a way that will be transferable to the saddle so that you get the same responses when you ride him as you do from the ground. You want the horse to increase in suppleness and to learn how to yield to requests from the reins and from the rider's legs.

>> **It is important with all in-hand work** to be quiet, calm and gentle. This will help the horse to stay relaxed and understand what we are asking much more easily. Under no circumstances must we give the horse the impression he is trapped between the fence, the reins and a mad-person with a stick!

Yielding to touch

If you think about it, many of the aids given by you are a request for the horse to yield to you in some way: the feel in the reins asks the horse to turn, slow, rebalance etc. by yielding to the bit; the touch of the legs asks him to yield by travelling forwards more or by going sideways.

>> **A horse who yields calmly** and with instant lightness to your touch is heaven to ride, and working on the ground is where you can begin to have the conversation.

Yielding the hindquarters

Firstly the horse should be taught to yield his hindquarters. This will be the introduction to the turn on the forehand and will lead to all kinds of other movements and responses to the rider's leg aids. You want the horse to step one hind leg across in front of the other hind leg for one stride.

1. Bend his head slightly towards you with the reins.

2. Touch behind the girth *very lightly* with your hand where your leg will go when you are riding.

3. Tap-tap-tap with the stick on the hindquarters to encourage him to step across. (If the horse does not respond immediately to the touch with

the hand – point 2 – the touch with the hand and the tap with the stick should be used simultaneously.)

4. As he steps correctly, cease asking and rub him as a reward.

5. Repeat a few times on both sides, keeping things calm and quiet.

Caitlin asks Quarme to move her hindquarters sideways and the mare obliges with a very clear step across, showing she understands the request very well. Cait's left hand holds the inside rein just four inches from the bit and asks for a bend. Her right hand holds the outside (supporting) rein, which comes over the withers, and also holds the stick which touches lightly on the horse's haunches to ask for the step.

>> **This is important to understand** – As a rule, if the horse's head is bending to the right, his body (shoulders and haunches) will naturally go left. And if his head is bending left, his body will go right. It is simple biomechanics.

The leg-yield

Once the horse understands to yield the hindquarters at the halt, it is not too difficult to develop the movement into what will become leg-yield when we ride.

1. Begin to ask for the yield of the hindquarters in exactly the same manner as in steps 1–3 above but as the horse lifts the hind leg from the ground, begin to walk very slowly across in front of the chest so that he also steps across – forwards and sideways – with his forehand.

2. Maintain the bend of his head slightly towards you – away from the direction of travel.

3. Take your time.

4. Keep the stick parallel to the ground and close to the horse's haunches to help him to keep stepping sideways as you both walk.

Fantastique in leg-yield, note the bend is slightly away from the direction of travel. I am walking slowly across in front of her chest. The stick is staying level with her haunches, passively encouraging her to keep stepping sideways. My left hand holds the inside rein four inches from the bit asking for a bend, the right hand holds the outside rein over the neck to control the outside shoulder and the amount of bend. The right hand holds the stick near to the haunches to ask the horse to move.

The rein-back

Rein-back is useful for all kinds of situations; it is a useful tool for our *lightness* training of the horse because it assists in roundness, collection and engaging the horse's hind legs underneath him, and rein-back can help soften the contact and is something we can use to develop the horse's response to yielding.

1. Stand to the side of his head, looking backwards towards his rear.

2. Pick the reins up lightly in up-turned hands, i.e. with your palms facing the sky.

3. Make a light action of the reins towards the horse's withers.

4. As soon as he takes a good step backwards, cease asking and let him know it was great.

Quarme in rein-back: Caitlin's hands are giving a feel in the direction of the horse's withers, asking her to step backwards and lightening her forehand a little at the same time. Cait stands to one side of the horse where she can see the whole horse, and all four feet in particular, so she can see exactly the quality of the resulting rein-back. Her hands hold the reins in a light feel and ask in a slightly 'up and back' fashion towards the horse's withers; this lightens the horse's forehand as well as asking for backward steps.

5. As he begins to understand rein-back well you can refine this exercise, making sure he stays straight and steps in a clean two-time rhythm with his feet as you request more steps.

6. Look for him rounding nicely onto the bit, arching his neck and lightening the forehand as he steps backwards.

If you have trouble getting him to understand rein-back with the bit, start out using a rope halter, to preserve the sanctity of his mouth. You may also find in the beginning it helps to say 'Back, back' and/or to tap him on the chest with a stick to help him understand the rein aid.

Neck reining

Even if you don't intend to ride western, it is useful to teach the horse to neck-rein so that you can control his shoulders and turns and help to keep him in balance with the outside rein on circles. Stand beside his neck with your solar plexus facing towards the front of his chest.

1. Pick up the rein nearest to you and place it against his neck.

2. Use your body language to encourage him to move his front feet one step sideways away from you by directing your torso towards his neck, so that he steps away from you.

3. If he doesn't understand, support the request by tapping his shoulder near the top of his leg or moving him over with your fingertips or hands on his body.

Following a feel of the rein

Whilst we have taught the horse to 'move away' by teaching him to yield his haunches etc., we can also benefit from teaching the horse to 'follow a feel'.

1. Stand in front of the horse, about an arm's length away from him.

2. Pick up one rein and open it gradually outwards away from his neck so that it leads his front end to one side and he takes a step across with his foreleg, effectively following the feel of the rein's invitation.

3. Relax and reward him.

4. Repeat both sides.

The Four Basics

...Have you ever found yourself looking into the horse's eye
and feeling disconcerted or emotional? ...at that very moment
your soul recognised the soul of the horse as part of your
spiritual family...

– Margrit Coates

In physical riding terms you could say there are only **four basics** you need
to be able to get a horse to do:

1. go forwards

2. stop

3. bend and turn right

4. bend and turn left.

That's it!?

Now here's the catch: you need to be able to do them all *brilliantly* – in any
combination, and that's where the hours of dedicated practice come in.

Let's explore some examples of that over-simplistic, crazy-sounding state-
ment that all you need is those **four basics**.

U.K. dressage star Carl Hester demonstrating nice forwardness and a
good bend at the same time.

- Imagine brilliant 'go' in trot and brilliant 'stop' at the same time: you could get piaffe!

- Imagine brilliant right bend, brilliant 'go' and a bit of brilliant 'stop' at the same time: you could get right shoulder-in.

- Imagine brilliant 'go' in canter, brilliant left bend and a goodly amount of brilliant 'stop' at the same time: you may get left canter pirouette!

The great thing about thinking of the four basics is that, at any given time when you are schooling your horse, it is reasonably easy to tell which of the four is lacking or needs to be improved the most, and when you work on the one thing that needs improving – the horse naturally goes better.

> **》 In any given moment** you can only really work on one thing at a time. By looking at how the horse is going you can usually decide what the most useful thing is to work on in that moment.

How to use the four basics

Instead of going round in ever-hopeful circles, a more intelligent approach to training is to look at which of the four basics outlined above needs to be improved, and then chunk down your training so that you work specifically on improving that one aspect of the horse's work. Let's look at some examples of how to chunk the training down and work on one basic at a time.

Example 1

The horse is in trot but rushing or leaning into the bridle.

Question: What is lacking?

Answer: The stop. So, come back to walk and practise some walk-to-halt transitions until they are great. Then ride trot-to-walk transitions until they are great. Then ride trot-to-halt transitions until they are easy. Hey presto; the horse has improved his balance in the trot.

Example 2

The horse is stiff in the inside rein (probably the left one) and looking out of the arena a lot too.

Question: What is missing?

Answer: Left bend. So, ride a left shoulder-in, or halt and ask him to flex his neck to the left in halt (making sure the right hand is not blocking the left bend); or ride some 6m circles to the left in walk and then maybe 8m circles in trot, in which the left bend will come more naturally.

Example 3

The horse is hard work to keep going and *your* legs are doing all the work, he lacks impulsion or needs more expression in his gaits.

Question: What is missing?

Answer: Going forwards. So, ride just half a 20m circle in canter then go **forwards** to trot; or ride trot, come **forwards** to walk for a *single* stride and then trot immediately again, repeating this a few times in exactly the same places in the arena so that he starts anticipating and going forwards of his own volition; or 'wish' for piaffe, (a trot which asks for energy but isn't allowed to go anywhere), and then suddenly – whoosh! – let him go forwards and see what happens.

Note Never 'take' too much work or energy from a horse who doesn't go naturally forwards very much, just ride for short sessions, and if in doubt get a good result then quit for the day.

From the above examples you should be getting an idea of how to improve the horse's work by focussing on which of the four basics is lacking and chunking down the riding to work on one thing at a time.

Riding Free

I'm here for the horse – to help him get a better deal.

– Ray Hunt

It is important to be able to ride the horse on a free rein with little or no contact. This is the horse's chance to stretch out, to chill out and to be trusted. It is a good way to start with young horses if you want to develop relaxation and a light response to the guiding rein aids. Even in higher-level dressage tests you are required to perform walk on a free rein, which means you have to show that your horse is relaxed, swinging and calm in the walk.

The reins are there for connection, to shape the horse and to show him what we want, not for control. If you cannot ride the horse without keeping him on tight reins then the reins are being used for control, and this negates the higher possibilities of what we are aiming for in our training.

I like to make sure I can ride a young horse on a loose rein before asking for too much with a contact, that way he learns to follow the feel and invitations of the reins as they open or close against his neck, allowing him to carry his neck in a lengthened and lowered position (a lowered head carriage naturally stimulates the release of endorphins, the relaxant hormones, into the horse's system).

>> **There can be few nicer moments** to share with a horse than trundling along in the countryside or on the beach on a loose rein, knowing you can trust and guide him, knowing he is relaxed and 'with' you and that you both feel quite happy in one another's company.

Carly guiding her horse on a loose rein, allowing him to chill out and stretch his neck.

Instead of *riding* the horse, give him a relaxed contact or slack rein and think of *guiding* him: it sounds like semantics, but the difference between riding and guiding the horse makes a world of difference. It also gives you a chance to relax yourself and check on the release of your own seat, neck, back, arms and legs. If you have a sudden emergency control situation, slide your hand briskly down the rein and bend or guide him more proactively to re-establish control – without surprising him, of course.

Willingness

...When I hear somebody talk about a horse or cow being stupid; I figure it's a sure sign that the animal has somehow outfoxed them...
— Tom Dorrence

Willingness is something that can be developed in the horse. It is also something that can be snuffed out by a lack of care in the way the horse is ridden, the amount of work 'extracted' from him or the structure of the work and expectations the rider has.

Ten points for developing the horse's willingness

1. Use intelligence to decide which exercise to do in each moment and how to juxtapose different exercises to develop your horse.

2. Let the horse know when he is guessing the right answer.

3. Remember that training a horse takes years, even if you are a total expert working with a perfect horse.

4. Have realistic expectations and adapt the work to help you and the horse realise those aims.

Willingness is not just important when working in the school. Horses should also be amenable to being ridden out, either alone or with companions.

5. Stop work while he still has 'gas in the tank' and is still mentally engaged enough to remember the lesson, preferably remembering it with a positive slant.

6. Be economical with your aids: use the lightest possible aids to get the job done and use them as briefly and sparsely as possible.

7. Vary the routine, ideally including riding outdoors (trail riding or hacking) and in the arena. **This is *really* important** to create an all-round well-trained, worldly and mentally balanced horse.

8. Only work on one thing at a time, don't try and 'fix' a range of issues all in one go – it will be too much for the horse.

9. Instead of thinking that training is about sorting out problems, think of it as looking for ways to help the horse go better.

10. Avoid using conflicting aids or giving more than one aid in any given moment. He can only really listen to one active aid at a time, so stick to this idea: **hands without legs, legs without hands**.

The Bend

Only the rider free from any contraction will have a horse equally
free. It is this total ease and relaxation that makes the rider as one
with his horse, without hindering any movements...

– Nuno Oliviera

When we talk about the bend of the horse we are usually referring to a
lateral bend of the horse throughout his whole frame, from tail to nose,
the bend usually corresponding to the inside of the circle or arena. The reality
is that the horse's spine is not naturally able to bend a great deal, although the
vertebrae in the horse's neck have lots of potential to bend, he can just about
turn around and use his teeth to scratch his own backside!

> >> **Anyone who has spent a little time** in the saddle will have
> noticed that horses find it easier to bend one way more than
> the other way.

One of the misunderstood myths of riding is that we bend the horse around
the inside leg by pressing the leg actively against the horse. Since horses are

naturally into-pressure creatures, if we press with the leg (with the idea of pushing the ribs of a 500kg animal around with our calf – ha ha!) the horse is more likely to lean on the leg than to yield his ribs away from it.

> >> **You will know when you have** the right amount of inside bend because the horse feels light, soft and *everything* works better.

Bending

To bend the horse around the inside leg only works if the head of the horse is bent correctly too. Lengthen your inside leg and confirm its presence slightly (well-forward on the girth) and the horse will take up the invitation to bend in his ribs, seemingly all by himself. The rider's outside leg stays passively behind the girth to *suggest* to the horse to continue the bend back towards his tail, but again there is little point in trying to wrestle a 500kg moving horse using the physical strength of your outside leg.

How to ask for the bend

How the horse is asked for a bend will vary a little from horse to horse, since some are naturally more flexible or more amenable than others, and also it will vary depending on whether you are riding the horse to the right or the left, since he will feel different on both sides.

- Have your inside leg lengthened and forwards at the girth (the horse cannot bend so easily further back in his ribcage).

- Ask with a slightly open inside rein, rather than the rein acting backwards or across the horse's withers too much: if the rein comes back towards your stomach it is an opposing rein and the horse is more likely to feel restricted and tense his neck rather than be light.

- Take a gentle feel and invite him to bend; wait for a response.

Young mare Quarme giving Caitlin a nice bend. Note the inside rein is slightly away from the neck (open rein) and the outside rein is in supporting position against the neck. (On a young horse it is not a problem to exaggerate that rein position a little).

- If the bend doesn't come from the light invitation, ask his nose to come a little further round, i.e. increase the amount of bend you are asking for even if just for a few moments, to obtain some softness.

- If the bend still doesn't come easily you could ask for a couple of lateral steps (leg-yield or shoulder-in) away from your inside leg; or you could do a small circle (6m or 8m), which will almost inevitably enable you to achieve a nice bend.

- Try turning your seat (hips) a little in the direction of the bend you want.

- Always be aware that the outside rein plays a supporting role and that it needs to yield enough for the horse to be able to answer the inside rein's request to bend.

Straightness

...A horseman of any tact will soon understand the modifications that he ought to make in their [the aids] application, according to the particular nature of his pupil (the horse)...

– Francois Baucher

Just like all four-legged animals, horses are not born straight. What we mean by 'straight' is that the hind feet naturally step in exactly the same tracks as the front feet, and that the spine of the horse follows exactly the line he is on, whether it be the curve of a circle or a totally straight line. You could add to this the requirement that the horse places equal weight in both shoulders and front feet as he moves, and pushes off exactly the same with both hind legs.

It is important to work towards straightening the horse so that he can work well in both directions and can collect and engage his hind legs evenly. Evidence that he is not straight might be things such as: he falls in or out on the circle, he leans on one rein more, he tips you to one side of the saddle, he finds it harder to turn one way than the other, he is difficult to strike off on both canter leads easily, etc.

> **» It is useful to know that your horse** is not naturally straight and which side of his hindquarters is weaker, stiffer or less mobile. It is more common for the horse to feel softer in the right rein and stiffer in the left because of their natural bend to the right. It is also more common for the left hind leg of the horse to be the weaker of the two, although that does not apply to all horses.

How to achieve straightness

- Really get to know the natural kinks in your horse: which ways he prefers to place his head, shoulders, ribs and hindquarters if you let him go along in his default position.

- Make sure the horse's nose is not bent too much one way or another. If he bends his nose too much – say to the right – his opposite shoulder will tend to 'fall outwards' rather than travelling straight in front of his hindquarters.

- Work in the **shoulder-in** a lot in both directions, so you can easily place his shoulders wherever you want.

- Avoid collecting the horse too much by compressing him with restricting reins and legs: if he is squished between the aids he is more likely to try and wiggle out of collecting by not going straight.

- Take the time it takes to strengthen his weaker, less flexible hind leg. It can take pretty much forever to help the horse in this way and is an on-going piece of work. Don't work more on the weaker side, but be aware that you are trying to develop that specific side of his hindquarters when working. Use circles of various sizes and lateral movements to build him up and help him become more even behind.

- Straightness is much aided by developing nice easy bending in the horse.

- Ride the centre line and quarter lines (5m in from the track) regularly to gauge accuracy and straightness.

Event horse Ginger showing a good example of 'forwards
and straight' across the long diagonal of the arena.

Balance and Collection

...We shall take great care not to annoy the horse and spoil his friendly charm, for it is like the scent of a blossom – once lost it will never return...

– Antoine de Pluvinel

Most of this book is about balance and collection. The horse is a four-legged animal whose natural centre of balance is nearer to his forelegs than his hind legs. Add to that weight distribution the encumbrance of the rider's weight and even more of the overall balance goes onto the forehand. So much of the work we do to make a great riding horse is to do with helping to shift some of that balance backwards towards the hindquarters, and like many things in riding, the correct solution sounds largely paradoxical: to get more weight back on the horse's hindquarters we ride forwards! Of course that isn't the whole story; we ride him forwards into a nice receiving contact, we help him to be free from stiffness and to be straight, so that his hind legs step honestly forwards underneath his body and lift him up in the middle, thus lightening his front end. This is done little by little over a period of years.

Every horse is a different shape and has a different way of going. Some horses have better natural balance than others and some collect more easily than others. What we mean by 'collecting' is that the horse steps well underneath his body with his powerful hind legs, arching his back and shortening his overall frame. Some horses have a natural tendency to carry more weight with their hind legs underneath them, and some horses tend to push with their back legs more than they carry. Ultimately we are aiming for the horse to become stronger and suppler so he becomes more capable of carrying rather than just pushing with his back legs.

How to improve balance and collection

- Spend years patiently working at the quality of your horse's way of going.

- Receive the forward motion into a *light* contact: a strong contact will not help the horse to find his balance – he will be using your hands to balance upon instead!

- Teach the horse to carry the bit in a light and correct way.

- Ride lots of quality transitions.

- Ride lots of quality lateral movements such as shoulder-in and half-pass.

- Ride up and down hills.

- Teach the horse to be very responsive to your legs and seat (see The Leg Aids and The Seat and Weight Aids): so that '... the horse quivers at the breath of the boot...' Pay regular attention to your own balance and seat in the saddle, making sure you help rather than hinder the horse's way of going.

The rider's balance

Because the rider is high up on top of the horse, the rider's balance has a magnified and huge impact on the overall balance of the horse. The tiniest lack of balance from the rider and the horse may find himself being toppled out of balance too.

1. Experiment with your balance point a little by allowing yourself to roll your upper body forwards or backwards or up or right or left, and

remember that it will need to adapt to the momentum of each moment in order to stay in agreement with the horse and the gait in which he is travelling.

Exemplary classical rider and author Anja Beran demonstrating beautiful balance and collection.

2. If you are truly in balance, the muscles of your whole leg – including the thighs – will be able to relax totally, as will your stomach muscles.

3. Keep looking straight ahead above the horse's ears – it will help you to feel where your correct balance point should be.

4. Look at how the horse responds to your balance experiments in order to know how to sit, rather than going with what feels normal to you.

5. When you are truly in balance it can feel like you are floating, a little light-headed even, and you can feel insecure in the saddle to begin with, since you are no longer holding on for security with legs or hands, or anything else for that matter.

>> **Make sure you carry yourself in** agreement with the forward motion of the horse and move together like perfect dance partners. Tipping your weight back to try to get the horse to take his weight back over his hindquarters doesn't really work. All that happens is the horse has to hang around waiting for the rider because the rider is going backwards; the horse is also likely to hollow his back a little, which is the opposite of what you are looking for.

Hands, Reins and Contact

By contact is meant a soft, steady connection between the
rider's hands and the horse's mouth...

– Carl Hester

We humans do just about everything with our hands, so it is not surprising that we tend towards using the hands too much and too actively when we ride. Ultimately, the hands, reins and contact are not there to *make* the horse stop, turn or come on the bit, they are just one part of the way we shape and guide the horse. The more passively the hands can achieve their aim, the better horses go. A rider who is described as having 'good hands' is one who appears not to be doing anything at all with the hands, i.e. the hands appear to be totally passive; aiming to ride in that way is a worthwhile goal for anyone who wishes for their horse to go beautifully.

The hands

The position of the hands (and arms) has a huge effect on the horse's ability to accept a light contact and find and maintain a good shape throughout his body. In neutral position the hands should naturally point towards the horse's mouth, with the elbows nicely bent so that the upper arms are almost vertical. This feels odd to many riders, especially if they want to give the horse a 'light contact' and have been holding or yielding the hands and arms too far forwards. In reality, the position I have described gives the rider the best chance of staying centred and also gives the horse the nicest feel in the contact, since a bent elbow is more able to absorb the movement between the horse's mouth and the rider's hand than a straight arm.

In general keep your hands still, especially the inside hand, and definitely don't be tempted to use them alternately to get his head down, even if everybody else at your yard does it!

Having the fingers closed and the thumbs uppermost helps the horse to have a consistent contact. The rider who can hold the reins without tensing the hand or inside the wrist joint will give the horse a nice feel in the mouth, which will be returned from the horse to the rider.

>> **Think of riding with your elbows** rather than your hands... and think of your elbows as belonging to your body, so that your whole torso connects with the horse through the reins.

The correct positioning of the hands and arms and the holding of the reins gives the best chance of a flexible feel in the reins for the rider and for the horse's mouth.

The inside rein

It is the inside rein, along with the inside leg, which asks for an inside bend. It is better to position the rein very slightly away from the horse's neck, to avoid compressing the horse's neck or trapping him between your hand and the bit – a situation that usually results in the horse bracing or resisting the request to bend.

It is not ideal to steer the horse with a dominant inside rein, as this tends to result in the horse bending his nose too much to the inside and falling out with his outside shoulder, or falling into the circle because the inside rein is pulling him in.

> **≫ Look for opportunities to relax** the contact on the inside rein regularly, e.g. when you are riding a circle and the bend is established, try releasing the inside hand forwards and seeing if the horse stays in the bend. Try the same thing with the inside rein during lateral movements; the horse will probably go with more fluidity and elegance.

The outside rein

The outside rein does a lot more than you might think.

- It filters how much bend is allowed by moving forwards towards the horse's mouth (to allow more bend) or not yielding forwards so much, in order to limit the amount of bend.

- It can be used to half-halt or rebalance the horse, by closing the fingers for a moment, or thinking 'back' towards the outside hip.

- It can be used to increase the degree of angle in a lateral movement by a slight increase in feel.

- It can help to keep the horse out on the track, but *only* if the inside leg and rein can maintain a good bend.

>> **Whilst it can help to have the inside rein** slightly open away from the neck, it is a good plan to try keeping the outside rein close to the horse's neck (except in the half-pass movements – see pages 152 and 166).

Contact

The aim of the contact is to serve as a connection between the horse and the rider. The contact should not be a means by which we force the horse into a particular shape.

The quality of the contact is the result of a number of factors:

- the way the horse has been trained

- the relaxation and willingness in the horse on that day

- the way you sit, the quality of your riding and especially how you have your hands and arms – even riding with your leg aids too strong can make the horse too strong in the contact by pushing him forwards into the bridle.

- the level of suppleness in the horse's hindquarters and in his back.

>> **Start out by holding the reins** at the buckle; then pick up the inside rein and then pick up the outside rein, so that you can just feel the horse's mouth on the end of both reins. See if you can keep that connection with him in your hands.

Of course the aim is to avoid having anything like a strong contact, as this would have nothing to do with lightness; equally if the contact is too light, and therefore inconsistent, it interferes with the horse's sense of flow, since the contact will be coming and going in his mouth like a bunch of on-going half-halts. Having a feel in the contact where the horse is steadily at one end of the reins and you are passively at the other, with just the weight of the reins between you both can be a very fine experience for horse and rider.

> **>> Look for relaxation in the horse's jaw** and neck by playing a little with the fingers of one hand. Yield the reins forward or even just relax *inside* the contact to discover more lightness of feel between you and the horse.

Note A constant contact is not really appropriate when using a bitless bridle (cavesson, bosal, side-pull, hackamore). They are designed to be used with a freer rein than the ordinary snaffle. The curb bit is also designed to affect the horse in such a way that it can (and should) be used without a constant contact, since the shanks and the lever action of the curb bit magnifies the pressure given by the rider's hand, as well as acting more on the horse's poll than does the snaffle bit. When using a double bridle it is a good idea to have the curb reins slightly slacker than the snaffle reins. It can be useful to try using a little more of the snaffle rein for the inside bend whilst using the outside curb rein to assist with the ramener, i.e. the shape of the horse's carriage.

Impulsion and Energy

Lightness through energy

– Julio Borba

Impulsion

What exactly is impulsion? Impulsion is the horse's willingness to 'go' in response to the rider's request. A horse who just wants to run like hell because of reactivity, adrenaline, habit or fear is not showing good impulsion, but simply being impulsive.

What you want from a riding horse is an immediate, available forward urge at the slightest request from the rider, no more and no less; *that* is impulsion.

Every horse is unique, and some horses lend themselves to offering impulsion more readily than others. At either end of the impulsion spectrum you will find horses who are naturally too energetic and horses who are too economical, and both types of horse can be challenging to ride. That is why it's important to pay constant attention to the horse's level of impulsion so that, with time and training, the horse will give himself over to us by offering precisely the amount of forward energy we ask for *when* we ask for it. With a less 'goey' horse that means being aware of the slightest slackening of his energy; and with an overly goey horse it means being committed to riding at our own tempo in every single stride until a happy agreement is reached between horse and rider.

>> **With time and correct training** most horses build their concept of impulsion so that a well-trained horse offers pleasing forward energy to the rider without question, but equally does not assume to flood the work with too much 'go'.

Energy

Generally speaking, horses possess energy in abundance. The question is whether the type of energy they express is appropriate for the work we are asking them to do, and whether the level of energy is right for our requirements.

To a large extent, skilful horsemanship is about knowing how to direct and control the horse's energy, and doing that starts with awareness of how much energy there is and what the horse is doing with it.

Jenny riding Ginger with good forward impulsion – a nice example of balanced forwardness.

How to increase the horse's impulsion and energy

- Rather than falling into the trap of working hard with constant strong leg aids, make light touches with a long stick on the horse's hindquarters – two taps each time – and use the stick at different volumes: tap-tap, TAP-TAP, tap-tap!

- Make lots of quick, clear transitions – really clear.

- Ride big patterns, big circles and straight lines. Make sure none of your turns are tight, since this has a braking effect on the horse.

- Canter a very short distance and then go into trot, taking the canter energy with you into the trot.

- 'Wish' for piaffe, collect the horse a lot, hold him back whilst asking for forwardness in trot, and then release his pent-up energy to go.

- Look ahead, above the horse's ears: ride as though you are going somewhere.

- Stop nagging with any of the aids (especially the legs) and pay more attention to the response to every single communication you have with the horse.

- Make sure you are sitting in perfect balance with the body relaxed and poised, and the hands, arms and wrists allowing and not blocking the contact. Make sure your hips, thighs and calves are loose and allowing him to move. Keep your heels off him; heels turned into the horse can restrict the horse's movement and it looks unattractive too!

- Ask him to really go for 40m, then stop and rest for a minute, then go again. The main thing is not to empty the gas tank by keeping pushing him around.

- Use polls, jumps, cavalletti, trail rides – *variety.*

- *Reward lots.*

How to decrease the horse's impulsion and energy

- Ride a small circle or figure of eight on very light contact or even longish reins, opening the rein to steer him. Reduce the size of the circles down to what they need to be for you to be able to control and direct the energy.

- Have your legs hanging passively and relaxed but in a quiet *constant supporting* contact on his sides.

- Sigh, smile a lot and stay calm. Maybe you could enjoy the high-level energy, but not too much – he may think that is what you want!

- Wait for the energy to settle whilst in the walk, making as small a pattern as you need to for him to relax.

- Ride some quiet patterns in the walk: 6m circles, shoulder-in, turn, half-pass and shoulder-in alternating and varying same on the other rein. Maybe make shoulder-in on the circle rather than along the fence.

- Stay 'in your body', stay very present and relaxed in your mind, being sure you relax your seat and fully 'be there' in the saddle with your 'full' bottom.

- Sit with at least two hectares of buttock on the saddle rather than clenching your bottom and perching above the saddle.

- Let your knees slide down the saddle flaps and soften the ankle joints.

- If the horse accepts being on the bit, fine. If he cannot, then try to keep the reins quite long, rather than an in-between length when he gets insecure about what you are supposed to be doing.

- Picture the horse relaxing and lowering his neck forwards and down in front of you quite clearly in your mind.

- Look above the horse's ears, rather than looking at him.

Tempo and Cadence

...In the trained horse, the desire for forward movement must be passionate and have the powerful rigour, the acute intensity of a permanent and imperious physical urge...
– General Decarpentry

Tempo

The tempo is the actual speed of the horse's footfalls. Tempo is related to impulsion but, whereas impulsion principally describes the amount of forward energy requested by the rider, tempo specifically means, 'What speed are we going?' Finding the right speed to work on any given day with each horse can be a skill in itself. What we need to find is a tempo in each gait that asks the horse to work rather than slack or rush, and a tempo that helps to train the horse to find a good overall shape and balance, which will give a light feel in the reins and a nice 'through' feeling in his body.

How to work on the tempo

- Try staying emphatically in the same tempo through circles of varying sizes, straight lines and changes of direction.

- Try working the horse in a slightly slower or faster tempo than that at which he wants to go; this can have the effect of getting him to work in a way which he may have managed to avoid if left to choose his own speed (which could have been either too fast or too slow).

- Try varying the tempo and see what happens.

- Instead of trying to make the horse go at the tempo you want, forget the horse and concentrate on yourself. If you go at the tempo *you* want with every fibre of your being, this will usually result in the horse picking up on *your* tempo and fitting in with you, which will mean you can maintain a far higher level of lightness in the aids.

- Try starting out at a relaxed tempo with the horse trotting in a nice balance and gradually increase the speed. When the increased speed causes him to lose his balance or roundness he is showing you it is beyond the capability of his natural rhythm and balance right now, so back off the tempo a little to find the relaxation.

- Be sure the vertical balance of your body is in *exact* agreement with the forward momentum of the tempo you require, e.g. if you want a good forward trot, it is no help to the horse to tip way backwards behind the vertical with the upper body.

Cadence

In equestrian terms 'cadence' means the amount of expression or 'lift' in the movement. This is something we will explore in more detail in Improving the Gaits. As with everything else, some horses have a naturally more cadenced action than others. Again, naturally occurring extremes of cadence, i.e. horse's action too high or too flat, can be more challenging for the rider.

If the horse is in a good rounded shape, moves with plenty of impulsion and you have control of the tempo you can start to ask for more cadence from the horse just by shortening the length of stride a little or by *thinking* 'up' more with each step.

Fiona's threen-year-old horse Relento demonstrating a high degree of cadence.

>> **The ultimate cadenced trot is called passage.**

Aids the *Light* Way

The 'mark' of the High School, of scientific, artistic, high
equitation, however one likes to call it, is not to be found therefore
in extraordinary movements, but in those, whether simple or
complicated, that are executed with perfect lightness...
– General L'Hotte

The aids are the means by which we *help* (aid) the horse to understand
what it is we want him to do. They are not a means by which we *make*
him do things.

The aids are *not* the message, they are the messenger; the message is the idea
we have about what we want the horse to do or how we want him to go. With
a clear idea in mind about what we want, we use the lightest possible aids to
communicate the idea to the horse. The instant the horse responds to the aid,
the application of the aid ceases.

It is important to understand that the horse is physically a highly sensitive
creature; he is also very mentally receptive, often seemingly bordering on extra-
sensory perception (ESP), or mind-reading. We can use these sensitive aspects
of his nature to apply the aids unimaginably lightly, and more often than not get
a greater response.

>> **TRY THIS Try riding 'by magic'.** That means riding some different patterns such as circles or transitions, without consciously giving any physical aids. Don't even turn your head or wish for it too strongly, just stay relaxed and allow it to happen. You might be surprised.

Intensity of the aids

There are varying degrees of intensity of the aids. It pays to start each application of the aids as quietly as possible. In between each of the stages listed below, a momentary pause can give the horse time to try to understand and respond to your request. Different types, individuals and breeds of horse vary quite a lot in terms of how long it takes them to respond with a physical response to the rider's aid.

The sequence of an aid

Remember to stop this sequence as soon as you get a response.

1. Think what you want.

2. Feel for the horse being in the right moment to respond, i.e. listening to you and in good balance.

3. Think about giving the appropriate physical aid.

4. Begin to let the aid imperceptibly breathe on the horse, either with your leg or a feel in the rein, for example.

5. Gradually increase the feel of the aid.

6. Wait for some kind of response.

7. Repeat the aid, e.g. tap-tap, or release and repeat the feel.

8. If it didn't work, rethink your approach and try asking in a different way.

Anja Beran showing a lovely example of absolute lightness of the aids.

>> **'Hands without legs; legs without hands.'** Use one aid at a time, and avoid giving conflicting aids simultaneously, e.g. hand and leg saying opposing things, or even right hand and left hand disagreeing with each other.

Never surprise a horse with an aid.

– Nuno Oliviera

The Keys to the Aids

...Only when the rider becomes quiet will the horse be able to hear the whispers of the fine aids...

– Erik F Herbermann

Make the aids as light as possible

The benefits of applying the aids lightly are numerous:

1. they don't interfere or block the flow of the horse's movement

2. they don't disturb the rhythm

3. they don't make the horse resist or 'push back' at you, e.g. the horse doesn't respond with 'If you pull, I will pull'; your position and relaxation in the saddle are not compromised

4. as with an artist's pallet, more subtle shades mean more things become possible

5. the lighter the aids, the more the horse listens

6. the horse is less likely to over-react to quiet aids, e.g. if the request for canter is loud the horse is likely to burst into a rough canter, if the request is quiet the horse will take a more civilised transition to canter.

The aids need to be well timed

This is far more important than most riders realise. When we give an aid we are asking the horse to give a specific response, and if we ask him at exactly the right moment in the sequence of his footfalls he will be able to respond more easily and with more lightness. If, for example, we want him to take a longer stride or a sideways step with a specific hind leg, we need to ask him to do that as the hind foot is leaving the ground, so that the horse can respond by following our direction with his leg. Another example is that of giving a half-halt with the outside rein: if we ask just as the outside foreleg is leaving the ground we can influence that leg to take a momentarily shorter or more elevated stride.

Of course this level of precision takes a little practice, but I can assure you it will be more than worth the time you invest in learning to dance the right steps at the right time with your horse.

The aid should be clear and precise

It is something of a miracle that two quite different species can communicate to such a degree that the one can carry the other and be guided so precisely. The only common language they share on a physical level is the aids. Consequently, there is no point trying to communicate with the horse in ways that might confuse him in an already confused situation! That is why the aids need to be clear, which means well timed – as explained above – but also precise in terms of where they are applied on his body, how long they last and how light or firm they are. In essence it is the rider's job to try to communicate with the horse in a way that makes the right answer seem totally obvious to the horse. When the horse receives clear messages that he understands he will almost always respond in the right way, because the horse is generally a compliant creature who just wants a quiet life. If you find yourself having to keep repeating an aid to get a result, perhaps the aid is not clear or precise enough or perhaps you need to think about how you can change the way you are communicating your wish to the horse, e.g. change the intensity, the rhythm or the location of the aid.

Clear and precise aids make the horse's job of understanding us that much easier.

An aid needs to be effective

If the horse doesn't respond to your aid, your aid failed to do what it says on the tin. The aid needs to elicit a response from the horse, and if it doesn't, you need to notice immediately and do something about it, such as ask in a different way, change your plan, get the horse listening more first, make the aid better timed or at a different intensity. The problem with allowing aids that get ignored to sneak through the net is that they quite quickly make the horse less responsive and dull, which is the opposite of the aim of your training.

Every aid needs to be given consciously

Follow this sequence for every single aid you give, *every time* you give one.

- *Think* what you want.

- *Think* how to ask.

- Give the aid.

- *Notice* how the horse responds.

- *Decide* how to follow up on the response the horse gave you: did it work?
  In which case go quiet with the aids to let him know he did the right thing.
  Did it not work? In which case try again slightly differently or take
  a different approach.

The Leg Aids

The legs of a supple-seated rider, which are in soft contact
with the horse, receive impulses from the oscillations of the barrel
(of the horse)...

– Waldemar Seunig

Many people talk about the need for lightness in the rider's hands, but there can be equal benefits to having a lightness of touch with the legs too. It can help the horse enormously if the legs are quiet, consistent and still. Think of the art of riding as a dance; can you imagine ballroom dancing with a partner who was kicking and bumping you all the time with their legs? To go forwards the horse needs to be able to expand and contract his ribs and undulate his spine, which is a good reason to aim for lightness of legs. Relaxed legs allow the horse's back to grow upwards and outwards, meaning he comes into a better outline and over-all carriage *with lightness* too.

There are many things you can do with your legs on the horse. In combination with other aids and exercises you can:

- support the horse

- ask him to go forwards

- increase the length of his steps

> ≫ **As much as possible, allow the legs** to drape down the sides of the horse. Release the legs well from the hip joints and have all the joints of the leg (hip, knee and ankle) as relaxed and flowing as possible. Remember, your legs go all the way from inside your hip joints down to the soles of your feet.

- withhold his forwardness, collect him or decrease the length of his steps

- make him more round

- ask him to step higher and with more elevation

- ask him to move sideways

- or even ask him to stop!

You can also use the legs to:

- 'listen' to what the horse is doing

- feel which of the horse's feet are moving at any given moment

- feel if he is giving you a good bend through his body

- feel if he is rounding up nicely from his stomach muscles

- feel whether he is relaxed or tense in his body and in his gaits.

There are many different ways you can communicate these things with your legs: squeeze, touch, tap, breathe, embrace, hold, release, brush, kiss, tremor, channel, allow, activate, sense, press, tickle, sensitise, support, instruct, stabilise, restrict, bend, withhold, shape, feel and listen to the horse.

In front of the leg

The phrase 'in front of the leg' means that when the rider touches the horse with their legs the horse instantly and willingly goes forwards. Some horses are naturally twitchy and go forwards from the leg with little training, but many horses need to be educated to be in front of the leg.

To teach a horse to be in front of the leg we need to use light leg aids and not fall into the trap of getting strong with the legs in order to push him forwards. Horses can feel a fly land on their skin, so it is quite natural for the horse to be able to feel a light touch; all we have to do is let him know that a light touch at the girth means 'go'.

> ≫ **It is important to be aware of what** your legs are doing at all times on the horse: if they are flapping, kicking or squeezing every stride without your knowledge you need to get them under control, because constant leg aids will only succeed in desensitising the horse's responses, reduce his impulsion, hollow him, bore him half to death or drive him crazy.

Emily is riding her sixteen-year-old ex-racehorse, Copper, with quiet and supportive leg aids.

>> **Using strong or squeezing leg aids** can actually have the effect of making the horse drag along. Strong legs restrict his ability to swing, coupled with which, a strong lower leg means the rider most likely has to have an equivalent amount of counter-tension in the upper leg, and that restricts the horse and rider's ability to flow freely forwards. Keep your heels from digging into the horse too. Imagine that dance partner whose legs were stiff as they pushed you around the dance floor, or who kept digging their heels into you! No thanks.

If the horse doesn't understand the light leg aid, touch or tap him lightly twice on the haunches with a schooling stick: tap-tap.

>> **Most horses are 'into-pressure' creatures,** which means if you apply pressure to them they are quite likely to lean on you. This is what happens if the rider's legs squeeze on the horse's sides enough that the horse can lean on the rider's legs with his ribs. This is the opposite of the response we want from the horse, which is to move *away* from light touches of the legs.

How to use your legs

Try some of these ideas.

- Slide your knees well down the saddle flaps to lengthen your legs and keep only a light pressure on the stirrup irons by softening your ankle joints – it can help round the horse through his back.

- Brush a few of the hairs on his side forwards very gently with your inside leg to ask him to step around a circle.

- Hold the horse in a gentle constant contact with both legs to encourage relaxation, throughness and forward motion.

- Hold the inside leg well forward and long at the girth to help with the bend.

- Touch very lightly with one leg (or spur) at the girth a moment before feeling the rein for more softness in the bend or contact.

- Imagine you can tuck your legs underneath the horse to create more lift.

- Momentarily press the thighs a little into the saddle, this can be part of a half-halt or a halt, it can rebalance the horse in trot, and it can help make the passage.

- Lift your legs off the horse then reintroduce them just an inch further back but very *very* lightly, for increased impulsion.

- Allow the legs to hang and swing with the horse's movement so that your legs can feel each hind and fore foot of the horse as it leaves the ground.

- Release the inside of your upper thighs and hips to allow the horse to go forwards more freely.

- Imagine the saddle is much bigger than it really is: release your legs and knees without taking them off the saddle – absolutely no gripping with any part of the leg – and see if it helps the horse move out with more expression.

- Take the legs way back for good quality rein-back steps, or for collecting the canter or to ask for piaffe – the legs way back ask for energy but withhold the forward motion a little.

- Lengthen your legs, place them on the horse at the girth and hold them there to make a halt.

- Rotate your legs around so the knees are facing towards the horse's muzzle – this can help to increase the quality of his steps and really open and round his back.

- Remember to relax your legs as much as possible; that includes keeping a lightly lowered heel with very little pressure on the stirrup iron.

The Rein Aids

...make yourself understood and let it happen...

– François Baucher

I am almost reluctant to write a section about the rein aids, because it implies we should pick up the reins and control the four-legged beast with them! We humans are extraordinary in the animal kingdom because we have an opposing thumb and have therefore evolved to do just about everything with our hands, which has ultimately lead to our supremacy over and impact on the whole planet. So, here we are sitting in the saddle with the reins in our hands, and what are we going to do with them to make the horse surrender to our will?!

>> **The good news is that reins and contact** are potentially a wonderful part of the circuit of connection and communication between ourselves and the horse, but the problem with the reins and hands is that so much can (and often does) go wrong.

It is always worth remembering that the horse's delicate mouth is on the other end of the reins from our hands.

For this section we will assume the hands and arms are all in the correct neutral position, which means the upper arms hang relaxed, almost vertically by our sides. The elbows have a good bend and the forearms point in a non-tense way towards the horse's mouth. The back of the wrist is straight, which is the best position to have the wrist joint free and flexible, the hands hold the reins with closed but not clenched fists and the knuckles pointing at the horse's mouth. The reins act as a continuation of the rider's forearm, wrist and hand which makes an uninterrupted straight line between the horse's mouth and the rider's elbows, and since the elbows are hanging beside the rider's body, the reins have actually become an extension of the rider's body. Wow!

> **When learning to ride,** much of what we assume and are first taught about how the reins work to control horses is quite the opposite of the truth, e.g. you may have already discovered that pulling the reins harder can actually make a horse run away faster, and you may have also discovered that pulling the right rein often makes the horse slide away even more to the left rather than making your intended right turn!

How to use the reins

There are variety of subtle nuances and options of ways to use the reins within the scope of good riding; we can hold, lift, open, soften, feel, release, still, vibrate, resist, relax, yield, and probably many things besides.

- Generally speaking , seek to have the reins and your hands 'parked' passively in front of you when you ride, simply functioning as another way of connecting you with the horse; rather than trying to control 500kg or 600kg of moving creature with two lengths of leather attached to his face.

- Try to use the reins only to assist with the bend and for helping to set the shape, frame and roundness (collection) of the whole horse.

- To turn a young green horse right or left can require more of a leading, open, rein but most horses respond better if the inside rein is not dominant in asking for a turn. This is because a dominant inside rein pulls the horse's head around the turn but disconnects his neck from his body and legs, which means he is more likely to fall out of the turn than step nicely around it. In essence we should seek to steer the horse's feet, not his nose.

- Since the reins have become a part of the rider's body when held correctly, by resisting with the body – perhaps by bracing the back or by changing the tone of the spine for a moment – the resistance is automatically transferred down the reins, without the necessity to pull or add extra pressure to the contact with a separate hand action.

- Whenever the opportunity arises, soften the contact – descente de main – especially in the inside rein and see if the horse maintains a good position and bend in lightness.

- Think of beginning circles and lateral movements with the outside rein. Just by increasing the feel inside that hand a little, and perhaps laying the rein a millimetre or two closer to the horse's neck.

The Seat and Weight Aids

The seat is the alpha and omega of riding.

– Egon von Neindorff

Using the riding seat to influence the horse is a much talked about subject, but in reality it is actually quite difficult for one rider to convey to another exactly *how* to do it; this is because the use of the seat needs to be incredibly subtle and largely falls into the category of 'feel.' Another difficulty is the fact that riding is a living art, where things change moment to moment; therefore the rider needs to respond and adapt fluidly with their seat from one moment to the next, which takes lots of mindful practice.

> » **The seat is the centre** around which everything is based. The seat aids play a key role in helping the horse with his balance, movement and understanding of what we want.

The foundation for influencing with your seat lies in sitting as well as you can in the first place, which means sitting in perfect vertical and lateral balance, with no need to grip with legs or arms whatsoever to stay on the horse. The seat needs to be free and mobile enough to move in perfect unity with the movements of the horse's back in all the gaits and through all the transitions.

>> TRY THIS **To find your full seat on the saddle,** place your legs up in front of the saddle flaps, this will really bring you onto the three-point base of your seat. Then try placing your legs back down so that your feet are below your seat without your seat changing its relationship with the saddle.

How to use the seat aids

- Try lengthening or shortening the forwards movement of your seat in the trot and canter to influence the lengthening or shortening of the horse's stride.

- Try spreading the seat more over the area of the saddle to help the horse fill out in his back.

- Try relaxing the back of your waist to help the horse be lighter in the contact and step better from behind.

- Try lengthening your neck so your head goes forward and up (whilst leaving the lower back relaxed) to create more roundness and to help with smoother transitions.

- *Think* of making your right leg infinitesimally heavier to turn right, or your left leg to turn left (weighting the seat will happen anyway, but shouldn't be overdone).

- Align your seat with whatever movement you are asking the horse to perform, e.g. if you are asking the horse to turn right, turn your seat the appropriate amount to the right in agreement with the circle you are asking the horse to perform. If you are asking for leg-yield, align the angle of your seat with the leg-yield.

- Make sure your seat is totally in agreement with the horse's movement for the gait in which you are riding (that means your seat is trotting when you want the horse to trot, and your seat is cantering when the horse canters). When you cease to make that movement or change to a different gait the horse has more chance of understanding you. That also applies to using the seat to go from a forward gait into halt.

- Try taking your body balance a little forwards or a little backwards to find out what helps the horse to go the best. It may feel weird to you, but if he shows it works, do it. He will show it by moving more freely, rounding and lightening to the bit, or ceasing to rush so much if he is the rushing type of horse. (It should be noted that many reasonably competent riders have the habit of tipping behind the vertical and when they are aligned forwards a little their horses invariably go *much* better.)

- Make sure you absolutely don't tip inwards on turns and circles with your upper body. You can help to avoid this habit by not turning your head to look across the circle – even though you have probably been told to do it. Just keep looking above the horse's ears: forever!

- Ease your inside seat bone a little forwards for canter; this helps the horse to find the angle for the canter through his back. Then think of your inside hip moving forwards in front of you with each canter stride.

- In the sitting trot, make sure you move with the horse's back, which is actually moving right-left-right-left with the side-to-side rocking of his barrel, rather than up and down, which is what a lot of people assume.

- Learn exactly how the horse's back moves in each of the gaits; then you can make the movement of each gait a little yourself, rather than sitting passively and letting the saddle toss your backside about. You could try closing your eyes (in a safe situation) so that you really feel what the saddle is doing under you.

The weight aids

Using weight aids is also a much-talked about subject among equestrians but, the fact is, sitting in perfect balance, whatever the horse is doing beneath you, is difficult enough, without messing around by tipping weight this way or that!

The key to using the weight aids to influence the horse lies in using them to a highly subtle degree. Over-use of weight aids can unbalance or interfere with the horse's ability to move and often results in the opposite result of the one you

Kate placing a tiny amount of weight down her inside leg encouraging Tilly to make a good turn to the right.

want. For example, too much weight in the right side of the seat will unbalance the horse and push him off to the left; a tiny amount of weight in the right will encourage him to step naturally to the right to stay under your subtly shifting point of balance.

During lateral movements it can be easy to end up with your weight on the side the horse is moving away from. This is also a technique used in some western riding to ask for side-pass, but to create lateral steps where the horse stays in balance with flow and rhythm, you need to take your body weight very slightly in the direction of the lateral movement **during each step**, otherwise you effectively get left behind and the horse has to twiddle his hooves and wait for you all the time.

It is a mistake to take your weight backwards or down to make a good quality halt or downward transition. If you do that, you push the horse's back downwards instead of it rounding, which makes him hollow and less likely to engage his hind legs underneath his body. Tipping backwards to create a downward transition often pushes the horse into his forehand and into the bridle, actually making it less easy for him to stop!

Auxiliary Aids

...The use of the aids is essentially the same in dressage as it is in outside or ordinary riding. It is however more subtle and discreet...
– General Decarpentry

In addition to the seat, reins and legs we can help the horse to understand what is required by using the voice, a stick, spurs, and by setting things up so that he gives the right response; we can even use the environment and outside influences as auxiliary aids.

The voice

The voice can be used to sooth the horse or help him to lower his energy level. Even sighing loudly can help. Using your voice to ask for another gait can help the horse to understand what you have in mind, should he not be clear about it, e.g. 'tr-ot on' or 'whoa', and the voice can be used as a reward to the horse, to let him know he is doing the right thing. Unless he is about to trample you to the ground, it is best not to raise your voice or shout at all around horses: it makes them edgy, but it also makes you appear afraid or weak as a leader. Ultimately we should aim to ride without relying on the voice at all, but with a younger horse it can help him to grasp what is required.

The stick

I like to use a longish stick (usually from coppiced hazel trees) when riding. This means I can touch accurately and very lightly on the haunches to energise or engage that specific part of the horse. It is not a good idea to use the stick as punishment, as the horse will either learn to be afraid and distrusting of it, or become immune to its effect. Carrying a stick and the reins takes a little practice, that's all. The reason the stick is valuable is that it can touch the engine itself (the hindquarters of the horse) and is therefore easy for the horse to understand its meaning. Also, if your legs don't get the forward response you want and you have no stick, you are stuck; with a stick you can follow up your leg aids consistently until the horse gives automatic forward responses to the leg aids.

>> **I often suggest using two touches of the stick:** the first touch draws the horse's attention to that area; the second touch says 'go more please.'

The spurs

The spurs are very useful for refining the aids of the legs to a highly subtle degree; they can help lift or round the middle of the horse and can make the bend around the leg better defined. It can be a beautiful thing to touch or lift just three or four hairs on the horse's side with the spur, the feather-like touch talking to this huge powerful animal, and feel him lighten himself in response to your subtle caress. It is not a good idea to use spurs if you don't have control of your legs, if you use your legs without knowing you are doing it, if you cannot sit with your heels off the horse and if you are trying to use

The spurs (if worn) should only act as a refinement of the communication between horse and rider.

them to make the horse go more. Aim to use the spur as sparingly as possible – you can think of having them on your boots without actually using them and the horse will often pick up your thought that the spurs are there.

Setting things up

There are loads of ways you can set things up to help the horse respond to you. This is what intelligent training is all about. In its most basic form, even something like asking for more forwardness at the beginning of each long side of the arena will help, as will: asking for more collection in the trot by trotting down a slope or away from home; knowing the place in the arena where the horse would like to stop and improving his responses to halt; using the corners of the arena to increase the bend and engagement of the inside hind leg; or, even, stopping with the horse one metre from the fence and parallel to the track, asking him to turn 180 degrees *towards* the fence and asking for canter before the turn is complete – this will place him into a very collected transition to canter!

Using outside influences

Taking note of your surroundings and the activities going on around you is another way of helping the horse to respond to your wishes, (provided you use them to your advantage!) If you want a sluggish horse to learn to have more impulsion, take him to a show or busy place. If you want to work with a tense horse, work in a totally quiet environment and only then gradually introduce him to distractions. You can use deep going to get the horse to be more active in his leg movements, canter on heather or through waves in the sea to get more elevation in the canter strides, and ride lots of turns around trees or bushes outdoors to get him really listening and turning with freedom and swiftness.

Flexions

Allow the neck to be free, to allow the head to go forwards and up, to allow the back to lengthen and widen...

– F.M. Alexander

Some horses are born naturally flexible and yielding, but not all. Horses who are tense, 'bracey' or stiff in their jaw, poll or neck can be helped to work more easily by the measured use of what can generally be referred to as 'flexions'. Flexing the horse to relax and supple his jaw, poll and neck is something that has been used by horsemen for millennia. It has been perfected and honed by some schools and classical masters over the centuries. That said, not every modern rider agrees with this approach to training as they think it means the horse will be worked from the front to the back and it makes the horse too soft and bendy! Personally, my ideal is that when I ask my horse to yield in any part of his body, in any gait, wherever we are and whatever we are doing, I want him to be able to respond easily and instantly and say 'Yes, no problem'. And that includes the jaw, poll and neck.

It is essential to remember that a horse is only in the correct shape when he is working from behind and the shape of the horse comes about ultimately by him working through from his hind legs forwards towards the reins. However, if the horse does not understand to yield to the reins in equal measure to his forward energy, all the rider gets is a horse who feels strong in the hand and pulls, or who goes along with his nose stuck up in the air, bent the wrong way or pushed out in front and down on his forehand. Please remember, therefore, that the flexion work described here is only a part of the package and is by no means intended to make the horse work from the front to the back. In the words of the great master Steinbrecht:

> ...All motion starts in the hindquarters. If therefore the flexibility of the hindquarters must be the ultimate purpose of all dressage training, this in no way means that lateral bending of poll, neck, and spine are unnecessary... Rather, the flexibility of these parts must first be obtained so that it can then be used as a means for the main purpose, namely to work the hindquarters...

How to practise flexions

As already stated, every horse is different, so it is important to work with the following exercises as necessary for your individual horse.

Extending the neck

Ultimately, when the horse is working correctly, he should shorten his entire frame from back to front by rounding himself up in the middle. This shortening of his frame should not come about by compressing his spine – a common sight created by trapping the horse between the rider's opposing or restrictive rein contact and strong legs. The horse's spine runs from the poll to the dock of the tail. It is a good idea to teach the horse to extend the neck a little from the ground as part of your flexion work. Don't *pull* the horse's head forwards, but make a feel in both sides of the bit and invite him to lower and stretch the neck forwards a little, releasing his poll and the vertebrae of the neck.

The jaw

If the horse is tight in his jaw or tongue we need to ask him for relaxation. This is not so easy if he is wearing a tight noseband, especially a drop or flash type, which clamps his mouth shut. At the very least, loosen the noseband sufficiently that he can 'talk' a little with his jaw and tongue. Now you can gently move one side of the bit around in his mouth a little, perhaps making a little circle with your finger on the bit until he relaxes on it. Alternately you could try placing a finger in his mouth where the bit sits (in the gap in his teeth, i.e. the bars, to avoid being bitten), and encourage a little relaxation.

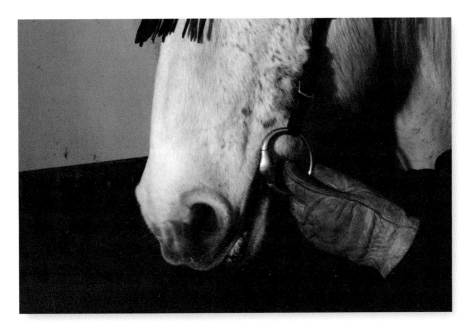

Helping the horse to relax the jaw and release the bit with a gentle feel of the hands.

The neck

Ask the horse to yield laterally to a light feel in one rein by inviting his head gradually around to the side. Wait until he softens in the contact and then release his head so he can straighten it. One side will feel stiffer than the other. Daily practice of this exercise will help horses with thick or stiff necks immensely and will eventually result in a much lighter response in the reins when you ride.

The poll

Ask the horse to bend laterally with one rein (as above) but this time only a few inches to the side, just far enough that he softens. Now hold that 'bending' rein passively and make gentle feels on the other rein with your other hand. When the horse yields by releasing at the poll and making a nice shape tell him he is great (in a quiet way) and then release him. Repeat this both sides. Done on a regular basis this will help the horse to understand how to relax his poll and give the rider a light feel in the reins with a nice carriage.

above Asking the horse to extend the neck, not by pulling the head forwards but by inviting the vertebrae to let go, thus lengthening the neck.

above right Developing lateral flexibility and freedom of the neck by asking for lateral flexion.

right Helping the horse to understand how we would like him to carry himself: relaxed and free from tensions.

Introducing Lateral Work

...You've got to be the change you want to see in the World...
–Mahatma Ghandi

...You've got to be the movement you want the horse to make!
– Perry Wood

The term 'lateral work' refers to moving the horse simultaneously forwards and sideways in a variety of specific ways. The benefits of lateral work to the development and lightness of the horse are many (this list is by no means exhaustive).

1. The horse improves his ability to bend both to the rein and through his body.

2. The horse becomes more flexible and supple throughout his frame.

3. The horse collects more by stepping underneath his centre of gravity with one hind leg or another.

4. The horse's straightness can be improved by making him more able to bend and therefore enable the rider to place each part of the horse exactly where they wish.

5. The horse becomes physically stronger in his hindquarters and his back by stepping underneath himself more.

6. The horse improves his balance, lowers his hindquarters and lightens his forehand.

7. The horse develops an independent response to each of the rider's leg, rein and seat aids.

8. The horse increases the extent of movement in the joints of his forelegs and hind legs when the legs are on the outside of the bend during lateral movements.

9. The horse becomes lighter to the aids.

10. The horse finds a rounded self-carriage more easily.

> **» There are a number of benefits** to performing lateral work for the rider, among which are a greater feel and understanding of each of the aids and how they can influence separate parts of the horse.

The classical gymnastic lateral movements include the shoulder-in, travers, renvers and half-pass. In addition to those movements you may include into the training such movements as turn on the forehand, leg-yield, walk pirouette, canter pirouette and side-pass (or full travers).

Turn on the forehand

To train the horse in the lateral movements it can help to begin with simple steps such as turn on the forehand as a way of helping him to understand to yield his hindquarters sideways away from the rider's leg. If you have followed the exercises in In-hand Work 1, you will already have taught the horse to yield his hindquarters from the ground so he should already have a basic understanding of it.

How to introduce turn on the forehand

1. In the halt, bend the horse a few centimetres to the left with the left rein. (The right rein can be in a position of support, to stop the horse from walking forwards, but obviously needs to allow the horse to bend left.)

2. Slide your left leg a few centimetres behind the girth and ask the horse to take one step sideways with his left hind leg, which should cross in front of his right hind leg.

3. Support the leg aid by a gentle touch on the left side of the hindquarters with the long stick if he doesn't understand what is required.

4. Walk a circle or two and then come to another halt. Repeat the exercise on the other side of the horse.

With training he should be able to do precisely the number of steps you ask for – not too many or too few – and to always cross in front of the other hind leg.

Solving problems

If the horse walks away forwards instead of stepping correctly, use your body or the reins to ask him to stay in place.

If the horse's hind leg doesn't step across in front of the other hind leg, think forwards as you ask, look ahead and make sure the reins are not too restrictive.

If the horse backs up or gets stuck, relax the contact a little.

> **» In general, don't be tempted** to use a strong leg to make him stop across in any lateral movements: if you set him up right he should understand the request and move from a light leg aid anyway.

Leg-yield

The next movement that can be useful in helping the horse and rider to understand the spirit of the sideways movements is the leg-yield. In the leg-yield the horse travels forward and sideways at the same time with the bend *away* from the direction of movement. Not all classical schools of thought approve of the leg-yield, but for a youngster to 'get the idea' it can be useful. It can also be a useful tool later on in your work, as a means to prepare the horse for some other movement you may wish to train. The reason for the disapproval of leg-yield is the risk of the horse being placed with increased weight on the outside shoulder/the forehand.

Carly and Murphy exploring leg-yield.

How to introduce leg-yield

1. Begin in the walk on the quarter line (the line which runs down the length of the arena midway between the centre line and the track – 5m in from the track).

2. Bend the horse's head a few degrees away from the track with the reins, keeping his body and legs parallel to the track with your own body and legs.

3. With the bend in place make a half-halt to slow the horse.

4. Slide your inside leg back a couple of inches to ask him to move his body sideways away from your leg. Time your inside leg aid to correspond with the moment the horse begins to step off the ground with his inside hind leg, so that you can influence it to move sideways instead of forwards. You can feel this moment simply by following the natural sway of his barrel towards the track you want him to move towards.

5. Maintain the bend and half-halt for each new step of leg-yield.

Solving problems

If the horse rushes forwards too much from your leg, make sure he responds to your half-halt, use a lighter leg aid.

If he doesn't move sideways you need to check that the angle of your hips is parallel to the long side of the arena, that you are looking in the same direction as the horse (bent away from the way he is stepping), and that the bend and half-halt are in place.

If he goes sideways too much, sit more evenly in the centre of the horse – not tipping right or left – and use lighter hand and leg aids.

If he loses the bend, open your rein a little away from his neck on the side asking for the bend, make a small circle, come around and start again.

The Gift of Transitions

The quality of a gait or exercise always determines the quality of the next gait or exercise...

–Arthur Kottas-Heldenburg

The term 'transition' refers to a change from one gait to another, e.g. transition from walk going up to trot, or canter down to trot. It can also refer to a change of pace within the same gait, e.g. transition from collected trot to extended trot etc. The benefits of asking a horse for transitions are many. Of course we need to teach the horse to go up and down through the gears just to have control of what he is doing, but transitions can give us much more than that. Transitions give us the opportunity to:

- increase the engagement of the horse's hindquarters

- round the horse through his topline (from his tail to his poll)

- increase his longitudinal suppleness

- tune him to listen more to our leg, rein and seat aids

- lighten the contact

- develop expression and 'spring' in his gaits

- readjust his balance.

The reason transitions are *so* good is that – assuming the horse doesn't lengthen his frame to make life easy for himself by pushing his nose out the front or trailing his back legs behind him – in the moment when he is going up or down a gear he is incited to step well underneath his body with his haunches. Over time this makes his hindquarters and his back stronger and more flexible. Transitions also lift and arch the horse's back, shortening his frame and increasing his overall power.

The challenging part about transitions is that we need to make them really *good quality* and we need to do *loads* of them.

Fiona's horse pushes upwards into trot.

The canter transition lowers Murphy's haunches and elevates his forehand.

What is a 'good quality' transition?

In a good quality transition, the horse responds instantly to our request and maintains the same overall shape or, even better, during the transition he becomes more engaged behind and rounds his back a little more. In a good quality transition the horse changes to the new gait with willingness and lightness, without dragging or rushing away, without pushing into the bridle, hollowing or ignoring the leg aids.

What do I mean by 'loads' of transitions?

I mean aiming to do perhaps hundreds of transitions in a schooling session. Making transitions is a better alternative than repetitively trotting round and round in the same way hoping the horse will go better at some point!

When and how to make loads of transitions

- If the horse is rushing, leaning on the bridle or not going at your speed, make some transitions to the next gait down until he rebalances himself and steadies up. If he is still pushing onwards, try going down another gait. For example, if he rushes in the trot, go down to walk a dozen times; and if he still rushes, try going to halt a dozen times.

- If you want the horse to listen to your aids more, ride a 20m circle and do as many as four transitions within each circle (one every quarter of the circle) until he tunes himself in to your legs, seat or reins (the arc of the circle should help to keep him more rounded through the transitions). This can be done by repeating the same simple transitions, e.g. trot-walk-trot-walk etc; or it could be a real mixture between canter, trot, walk, halt and rein-back, choosing whichever gait is going to help the most in any given moment. Play with it to get a feel for which this is for your horse on any given day and work around whichever gait you want to improve the most.

- If the horse is sluggish, e.g. in trot, put in quick transitions to walk or canter and back to trot again to enliven him.

- If you want to increase expression or spring in the trot or canter, make lots of upwards transitions into that gait: your first few strides after the transition will have more zing and elevation in them.

- Another way to improve the expression or spring in a gait is to do lots of transitions within the gait, e.g. make a *clear* transition to a bigger trot and then a *clear* transition to a shortened trot alternately: do that a good few times and see what happens (it should get easier with repetition). If you take this to its ultimate conclusion the shortened trot will become piaffe or passage and the bigger trot will become the extended trot. You can do the same thing within the canter too, shortening it as much as you can and then lengthening it out, again making the transitions totally clear moments of change.

Upward Transitions

Lightness! Agility! Balance! Those essentials of the classically trained horse were as relevant two and a half thousand years ago as they are today...

–Sylvia Loch

1. Prepare in your mind what gait you want next and how you want it to be.

2. Wait until the horse is in the right moment of balance to respond easily and gracefully.

3. Decide exactly what speed and 'flavour' of new gait you want in your mind before you ask. The clearer your mental picture, the lighter your actual physical aids can be. He may surprise you and do the transition without you being aware of giving any physical aids whatsoever!

4. Think; release yourself to go; light legs; touch with the stick; stay soft in the seat and remain in balance with the new forward gait. Hands remain where they can best help the horse to stay in balance, (probably in about the same place as they were before the transition).

Don't chase the horse for the new gait, ask as lightly as possible – you can always repeat the transition to refine it when he knows you are playing a game of upward transitions together.

Engraving from A *General System of Horsemanship* (1658) by William Cavendish, Duke of Newcastle.

We want upward transitions to be crisp, but not jerky. If you surprise the horse with a sudden or strong aid to 'go' he is more likely to rush away, push into the bridle, stick his head upwards and hollow his back downwards, and they are all the things we don't want.

Be sure that all of your aids agree with each other, e.g. don't give an inadvertent little pull back on the reins or brace in your back at the same moment as asking him to go forwards with the legs. Equally, don't ask him to go with your lower legs and then hold onto him with your thighs or heels.

Apply the lower legs in short, light touches. If the horse doesn't respond, avoid pushing hard with your seat or banging with your legs, instead give a couple of polite touches with the stick on his hindquarters to help him understand what the light request from your leg actually meant.

> >> TRY THIS **Try releasing or relaxing** the top of your inner thigh as a way of initiating an upward transition, it will release the horse to go forwards and give more space for his back to expand too.

Try to avoid throwing the hands forwards when asking for an upward transition, it may not help and may make the change worse by altering the horse's balance just at the wrong moment. This is especially something to watch out for when asking for a transition to canter.

You can refine and sharpen up the transitions to a new gait or to a bigger stride in the same gait by repeating the transition a few times. Do the transitions in the same places every time at first so the horse starts to anticipate what you are going to ask, which means you can be much lighter with the aids and concentrate on the quality of his shape etc. as he goes into a new gait.

Remember to look over the horse's ears for an upward transition; otherwise he may not understand your desire to go (he is less likely to understand the aid to go if you look down).

> >> TRY THIS **Try just *thinking*** of your head going **forwards and up** whilst making up and down transitions; it can help with the roundness and quality.

Make sure your upper body moves forwards freely in the correct balance with the new forward motion of the horse. This will help him to stay round in his back, go forwards more easily and give him more space for his hind legs to engage underneath his body mass.

Avoid pushing with the seat to go up a gear, especially into canter; it creates tension in horse and rider and hollows the horse in his back. Instead move fluidly from one gait to the next with your seat (remember each gait requires your seat to move in a different way).

> >> **I have noticed that, when the rider clucks** with the tongue, although most horses go forwards more, they almost all raise their neck in a tense fashion. If you feel the need to cluck your tongue for an upward transition, see it as a sign that your forward aids are not working well enough and you need to teach the horse to be more in front of the leg and more responsive to leg and stick aids.

Downward Transitions

...His back should be soft and swinging, his hind-legs engaged according to his stage of training, so that the body, neck and head appear to connect as a whole...
– Heather Moffat

1. Prepare in your mind. Think *forwards* to the next gait, even though it will be a lower gait than the one you are in.

2. Keep your balance, don't slump down, sink or stiffen your back. Avoid blocking the horse with the reins too.

3. Pick a moment when the horse is listening to you and is in the right attitude and balance to be able to change gear easily (that means when he is listening and not rushing forwards, tense or unbalanced).

4. Think about his feet going in a different sequence and the rhythm of the footfalls in the new gait, e.g. coming from canter: 1-2-3, 1-2-3, 1-2-3, goes forwards into trot: 1-2, 1-2, 1-2, 1-2.

5. 'Live' the new gait with every cell of your body.

6. Quietly invite the horse to join you in the new gait with your seat, and give a feel in the reins if necessary.

It is better *not* to actively pull both reins to make a downward transition, it can make the horse pull more, or hollow and stick his nose in the air. If active rein aids are needed it can help to keep one rein still (perhaps the inside rein, which passively maintains an inside bend) and make an active feel in the other rein (the outside rein gives half-halts or 'feels').

>> **Try not to rely on pulling the reins** for downward transitions: the reins are for the shape of the horse and the bend and connection.

Repetition and refinement work hand in hand to improve the understanding and quality of the downward transitions that you and the horse make together. And you need to give him time to make the transition down too, which means

Repeated downward transitions are a good way to create more lightness and to improve the contact.

preparing in your own mind an adequate amount of steps prior to when you want the transition to actually happen. It is better that the transition happens a couple or three steps after you wanted it but with good quality, than to force a rough performance for the sake of accuracy.

>> **TRY THIS To enhance the ability for horse** and rider to feel downward transitions, do many walk–halt–walk–halt transitions (halt every six or eight strides of walk) until they are so good you don't know what you are doing to get them, but you know both you and the horse have the feel of them. That is what you need for all downward transitions. By repeating the walk–halt exercise you will tune the horse in to respond to the subtle signals from your mind and body to change down a gear. Once that is happening like magic, do the same kind of thing for downward transitions from all the other gaits.

>> *Do not tip backwards for downward transitions.* Although you may see lots of riders doing it, the effect it has on the horse's back, and therefore his shape, is not what we want to achieve. Tipping backwards puts pressure into the horse's back and makes him inclined to hollow; it also pushes him into the forehand, makes him keep going forwards for more steps than he might otherwise take or come above the bit.

Using the School Patterns

'...lack of communication with horses has impeded human progress,' said Abrenuncio. 'If we ever broke down the barriers, we could produce the centaur.'

– Gabriel García Márquez

What we refer to as 'school figures' or patterns are really useful tools to use if you want to make a fantastic job of training your horse. The patterns have developed over the millennia to help us to better train a horse to be a responsive, supple and powerful ride. Making good use of the school figures requires some understanding, practice and intelligence; the rider who can use just the right school pattern at the right time could be said to be an intelligent rider. There are many pointers in this book to help you learn about what to ask and when.

School patterns and what they're good for

On the following pages is a summary of the most common patterns and some of their benefits.

Riding circles and school patterns with curves in them help to engage the haunches and strengthen the horse.

Circles

Circles can be anything from 6m to 20m in diameter. **Good for**: rounding, collecting, softening and achieving bend, placing the horse's inside hind leg under his body.

Straight lines

Straight lines can be ridden along the outside track, centre line, quarter line or long or short diagonals across the arena. **Good for**: increasing forwardness, testing out straightness of horse, increasing impulsion.

Figures of eight

The two circles of this pattern can be anything from 6m or 8m up to 20m in diameter. **Good for**: keeping the horse's mind focussed and increasing his ability to change bend and flexion throughout his body.

Serpentines

The full or half width of the arena is used for this pattern which can have a different number of loops depending on the horse's ability. (Fewer loops are less demanding, more loops are more demanding.) **Good for**: keeping a horse guessing and his mind open to what is happening, increasing flexibility and ease of changing bend and direction.

Spirals

This pattern starts with a 20m circle which is decreased gradually to as small a size as the level of training and the gait allow. The circle is then increased gradually or the horse is moved laterally (leg-yield) back out onto the big circle. **Good for**: increasing engagement of the hind legs whilst maintaining the same tempo, bend and impulsion.

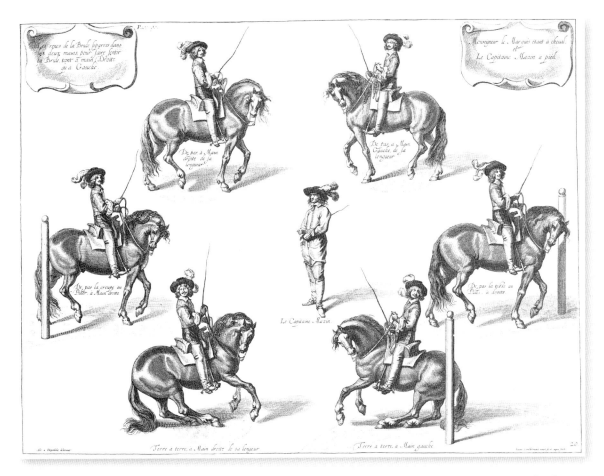

Squares

The smaller the square or the more angled the corners, the more challenging the exercise. (A right-angle turn in canter is a quarter of a canter pirouette!) **Good for**: straightening the horse and for achieving maximum collection on the corners.

Engraving of William Cavendish, the Duke of Newcastle, performing school patterns.

A typical schooling session

Depending on the horse's level of training, a typical session might include some of the following.

- Walk on long rein.

- Rising trot on both diagonals to warm up on 'friendly' contact (yes I know, all contact should be 'friendly,' but you get my drift).

- Smaller circles and lateral movements in collected walk.

- Lateral movements in trot and increase and decrease of pace inside trot.

- Collection and extension in both walk and trot.

- Canter on both leads – including circles of different sizes.

- Collection and extension in canter.

- Transitions in and out of canter

- Perhaps some lateral movements in canter and flying changes.

- For an advanced horse, piaffe and passage; for a less advanced horse pick something great to finish on, maybe a 'wow' trot.

- Relaxing walk to cool down.

Remember to give the horse rest periods regularly during the schooling sessions. Look for the tiniest moments of improvement and allow the horse to rest, so that he learns by the cessation of the work that he has done the right thing.

A word about accurate riding

Ultimately we want to ride totally accurate patterns on the horse. By riding a perfect circle, for example, we can be sure that the horse is bending, balancing and using himself in the most beneficial way.

It is perhaps more important during training to ride the horse in a good shape, rather than riding a circle accurately but sacrificing the horse's outline, correctness of the bend or correct application of the aids. This piece of advice also applies when you are working on the outside track, or along the wall or fence of the arena.

The Four Keys to Schooling

The definition of insanity is to keep doing the same thing and expect a different result.

– Albert Einstein

Have you ever found yourself trotting round and round in circles hoping the horse is going to go better? I think most of us have done it, but generally speaking it doesn't work very well.

What to do, where to go and how to use the school patterns in the arena can be a great mystery to many riders.

> >> **This may sound ridiculously simple,** but the answer to improving performance is this: **do more of what works and less of what doesn't!**

The four keys

1. **Observation** Observe the horse and look at exactly how he is going.
   Look honestly at what is working and what is not. Look at the actual

reality of what he is doing. That doesn't mean making stuff up about what he thinks or feels, e.g. 'He thinks circles are boring.' Avoid making assumptions and just look at the facts: is he rushing or dragging his feet? Is he stiffer on one rein than the other? Is he loading more weight onto one shoulder than on the other? Is he less active with one of his hind legs? Does he ignore your legs, perhaps one more than the other and, if so, which one? Is his head too high or too low?

2. **Intelligence** Once you see exactly how the horse is going, decide what you would like to change and think about what you might do to create that change. Remember that embedded changes and training of the horse can take a long time, but you should see some positive feedback immediately if you hit on the right approach. If you can't think what options you have look through the pages of this book, it is full of ideas about what you can do with your horse. (For a quick reference see The Four Basics).

3. **Experiment** If you are not sure what to do to get the result you want, just **do something different: experiment**! Even great riders don't know the answer for every horse every time until they experiment. Try changing some little things to start with: try changing the gait or the size of the pattern you are riding, try some lateral steps, try positioning the reins differently by an inch or two, try yielding a leg or rein, try relaxing in your body somewhere, try lengthening your legs, try increasing or decreasing the bend, try looking somewhere different with your eyes. The possibilities are endless.

4. **Evaluate** Some people are not very good at seeing when things go well, they just focus on the 'problem' and see how badly it is going all the time. This is not helpful. Unless you and the horse see what is working how can you possibly recognise what you should do more of? Try to stay objective about what result each little change or experiment produces: the horse will give you the clues you need to find the right answer, you just need to remain openly observant and see what the horse gives you by way of response to your experiments.

Ways to try doing something different

- In general, a smaller pattern or circle will slow or collect the horse, whilst a bigger pattern or straight line will increase the pace.

- Flexions, downward transitions, halts and lateral steps can unlock many of the resistances horses offer us.

- Making a large number of transitions or changes of pace within the gait can yield great results. (Just repeat the transitions a good few times and trust the process).

- Every change in the position of your body, legs or arms, and every internal adjustment of tension or relaxation in your body will change the result.

Emily using a turn to help Copper to bend and be soft. Aim to always know why you are doing a particular movement or pattern in the arena and what you want to achieve.

Murphy is a young horse with lots of power and enthusiasm in the canter and so working on circles will gradually help him to balance and use himself more efficiently.

>> **The first master I studied under** used to say almost nothing in the lessons except this: 'Sit well, do nothing and the horse will do.' Keep bringing yourself back to the fact that the way you sit in the saddle can be of transformational benefit in your schooling and shaping of the horse.

The Rein-back

...As the blind person touches the object before him very softly and lightly with his fingertips in order not to interfere with the work of the sensitive nerve ends by too much pressure, so it is the rider's first obligation to keep soft and natural those parts of his body with which he feels his horse...

– Steinbrecht

In the rein-back the horse should step in a diagonal two-time rhythm the same as for trot, with the diagonal pairs stepping cleanly and not dragging. The horse should stay totally straight when he makes the rein-back otherwise he is avoiding the optimum use of the hindquarters.

The rein-back has more uses than just being learnt for a dressage test or opening and closing gates, although those things may well be high on your to-do list. Rein-back can also be used:

- to help the horse round through his back and soften in the bridle

- to lower the haunches and engage the hind legs

- to lighten the horse's forehand

- as a precursor to asking for wonderfully collected canter departs (transitions to canter)

- as a preparation for piaffe.

Quite a list! That said, I am not recommending you spend your riding sessions with the horse going backwards all the time. The practice and training of rein-back needs to be kept in proportion and done with delicacy and thought. There are various methods of asking for rein-back, all of which may result in the horse going backwards in some fashion or other, but to gain all the potential benefits from the rein-back it is important to ask for it in a good way.

How to ask for rein-back

We have already visited rein-back from the ground and the horse is now familiar with the concept that we can ask him to go backwards; now we will ask for the rein-back from the saddle, refine the request and reap the benefits.

1. Come to a nice halt with the horse listening and waiting for your next requirement.

2. *Think* about rein-back and picture it in your mind. The power of intention should not be underestimated when looking for light responses in the horse, especially for movements such as this, and once he has learned the rein-back in the manner described here, intention will often be enough to initiate the movement!

3. We will aim to achieve the rein-back more with the legs than with the reins so that the movement results in maximum engagement and collection. To achieve that aim, begin with a light contact in the reins – just enough to passively stop the horse from walking forwards. You can try positioning the hands perhaps an inch or two higher than usual and turning your fingernails up towards the sky a little.

4. Bring your upper body *very slightly* forwards as though suggesting to the horse that the door is open behind him, but maintain your full seat contact with the saddle.

Kate's Arabian mare Tilly concentrating hard as she performs the rein-back. Notice the muscle tone in her haunches from doing this movement.

5. Move both legs quite a long way back behind the girth and place them as lightly as possible on the horse's sides. This will initiate the horse's feet to move, and since your legs are well behind the girth they will encourage impulsive activity without much forwardness: they will also help to engage the hind legs underneath the horse's body. Your passive contact lets the horse know that forward movement is not an option, so he chooses to go backwards, lightly and beautifully.

6. As soon as he initiates the backward steps relax the feel in your hands so that he steps back with more freedom in his movement.

7. To end the rein-back, bring your legs gently forwards to the girth, look ahead and take your body back into the upright position.

8. If you want to go on into a lovely trot or canter, it won't help if you throw the reins forwards to end the rein-back because the horse's balance will be dropped onto his forehand and he will find it more difficult to make the upward transition, so keep him in shape as you go from rein-back to an upward transition.

To improve the rein-back steps you can:

- give little touch-touch aids with your legs in time with the rein-back steps

- try touching very very lightly with the stick on the horse's haunches for more roundness and rhythm during the rein-back

- make a floating, vibrating feel in the reins to add to the lightness in the front.

Remember to train the rein-back well enough that the horse is willing and able to do it beautifully, but if he keeps anticipating, you need to drop it for a little while. In the beginning you may want to ask just for a couple of steps, so that he learns and understand the movement. Once he understands you can expand it to maybe four or five steps.

Sometimes go immediately from the rein-back into walk, trot, canter or piaffe, and sometimes perform rein-back and stop for a minute or two, so that the horse learns to sit back on his haunches and not think of rushing forwards all the time.

>> **Many horses don't go straight backwards** when reining back; instead they slew their haunches out to one side. The side they slide out towards is the side on which the hindquarters are weaker, so it makes sense for them to avoid placing their body-weight over that weaker, stiffer hind leg by putting it out to the side. To straighten the horse, do not use your leg to push the hindquarters back into alignment, but move the horse's shoulders sideways by shifting both hands a little sideways to realign his front end with his skewed back end; that way you are not just straightening him, you are also adding to the horse's state of collection (this is similar to how the shoulder-in works).

Developing a Good Outline

...you will see it is an excellent thing to have a gentle hand
(it is one of the greatest secrets we have in managing a horse)
even so to sometimes let it be quite slack...
– William Cavendish, Duke of Newcastle

There are a few terms you can use to describe a horse working in a correct shape: 'in an outline', 'on-the-bit', 'self-carriage' and 'round' are some of them. What is precisely meant by the horse being in the right shape will vary somewhat depending on the natural conformation of the horse and his stage of training.

In the right shape the horse should be stepping well forwards underneath his body with his hind legs, his back should be lifted, his face should be just about vertical, his stomach muscles toned, and he should be reaching forwards with lightness into the bridle with his neck arched and beautiful. Being in 'self-carriage' means all of this happens without the rider *forcing* it to happen or holding it all together with strong reins and legs, since that would mean the horse is not rounding himself but being squashed into an imitation of the ideal by the rider.

Anja Beran has this horse stepping well under his body with his hind legs, his neck is arched and his whole frame gives the impression of contained power in lightness.

>> **Contrary to common belief,** the correct outline is not something which is forced upon the horse with hard hands and driving legs, although some people do appear to be quite successful by following that route. Rather, the correct outline is something which we help the horse to find by gradually educating him to accept the aids and to go forwards confidently towards the bridle.

Push or carry

The horse can use his hind legs in two ways: either he can push forwards with them or he can carry with them. Most horses use their hind legs to push the majority of the time, but to collect and carry the weight of a rider the hind legs need to be developed to carry rather than push.

The benefits of a good outline

- The horse becomes much more responsive to the aids.

- The horse's working life should be extended because he is using himself more correctly.

- He carries you with smoother movement through his back, so he is easier to sit on.

- He feels great to ride!

- He moves better: more expressively and elegantly.

- He looks great!

- He makes optimum use of his whole structure.

How a good outline should *feel*

When the horse is in the right shape he feels smoother in his movements, carries you up on a nice strong back and is more sensitively responsive to all of the aids, especially the seat. He feels 'fuller', bigger and more powerful beneath you and more attuned to you with his mind, focus and attention. He will feel light and consistent in the contact, ideally giving you just the weight of the reins between you and him. He will feel like he is dancing across the ground (or even above it!). Nice!

> >> **Not everyone realises this** but being in the correct outline is very much a mental state for the horse, a state of acceptance and willing submission, when he hands his physical powers over to you completely. It is mentally relaxing for the horse to work in this accepting way, because he no longer has to take responsibility for anything other than following your directions and staying connected with you.

above Kate encouraging Tilly to reach forwards towards the bit.

above right Murphy raising his poll as a result of stepping well underneath himself from behind.

How to achieve a good outline

There are quite a few ways to assist in developing an outline, some work better than others depending on the individual horse. With time, patience and feel you should soon become quite adept at feeling for how each horse can be taught to 'seek' an outline. Almost everything in this book is about this subject and by following the ways of working described in its pages your horse should develop and sustain a very nice outline as if by magic. Try some of the suggestions below to see what helps your horse the most, either to find a correct shape or to maintain it as you ascend the levels of the work you do with him.

- Be committed to having the horse's full attention at all times (see The Attentive Horse) when looking for roundness: remember being on the bit is mostly a mental state of acceptance for the horse.

- Ride the horse well forwards into a light receiving contact, not rushing but moving with nice brisk gaits.

- Be sure the horse is going at the right tempo – not too slow and definitely not too fast.

- Use a slight lateral bend to the inside through his whole length: as you ride a circle, make sure he is bending nicely in the bridle and around your inside leg, **placed at the girth**, and not too far back.

- Try very very gentle touches of the stick, or resting it on the side of his haunches to engage the inside hind leg, but *not* so that he speeds up.

- Sit as well as you can – poised but relaxed and not trying too hard.

- Support him with the same light constant contact in both reins and both legs.

- Try releasing different parts of your body internally. For example, relax your lower back, relax inside your forearms, release your inner thighs etc.

- Understand the importance of engaging the horse's hind legs under his body; you can do this in a number of ways: loads of quality transitions are a good start.

- Use lateral steps or smaller circles, these engage one hind leg at a time, so when you've worked on both hind legs separately it will be easier for him to engage both hind legs at the same time.

- If necessary, teach the horse to be polite in the contact and not stiff in his front end by practising flexions. Do the same thing with his rear end, making him flexible by asking him to yield his haunches sideways with your legs.

- Make sure you train the horse to go forwards willingly, in front of the leg.

- Whichever side the horse finds it easier to create a correct shape (right rein or left rein), begin on that easier side, then go to the difficult side and then return to the easy side again when the difficult side gets too 'sticky' or stiff. Repeatedly going from the easy side to the difficult side will eventually even the horse up and help him to feel good both ways.

- Some horses hold too much tension in their front, which makes finding an outline more difficult, especially on one side. Starting in the walk, ride along the long side of the arena with the horse's legs and body going straight and bend his head a few inches to the outside by inviting with the outside rein (you know when it's the right amount of stretch or bend because he should feel light and released in the rein), then go straight. Do the same again, now bending him a good few inches to the inside. Then repeat the exercise (bending to the inside and outside) on a big circle; when he softens to the request for the bend release his head and allow it follow the true line of the circle. You can do all of this exercise in trot too.

- For a horse who is tense about the bit (or ruined by, or reactive to, the bit) try riding him with a light contact and imagine the bit is going forwards just in front of him all the time, so that it *imperceptibly* keeps escaping him by constantly moving forwards a fraction. Do this escaping-bit thing *within* the contact; that means the contact itself is not thrown away. Many horses really like this way of finding an outline.

Ex-racehorse Copper can be tricky about giving a good bend, so Emily is using some gentle stretches to help him unlock his forehand a little.

The Half-halt

...a World of "lightness", art, beauty and pleasure! To ride a horse is to feel all this and more...

– Luis Valença Rodrigues

There seems to be a lot of confusion about the half-halt, but we don't need to make it complicated – it is exactly what it says it is – it is a half of a halt! The half-halt can:

- rebalance the horse

- bring him into a better shape

- check his speed

- lighten his forehand

- lighten the contact

- prepare him for any change of direction, speed or new movement

- help him to listen more.

How to do a half-halt

Here are some ideas of things to play with to achieve half-halts. Every horse is different and every moment is different. Some days half-halts may happen as a thought, a whisper, a breath on the horse, other days may require a more proactive set of aids. This is what the rider must learn to feel with awareness and experience.

- Think of **halt**, and the split second the horse feels like he is about to halt, change your mind and continue riding forwards.

- Try lengthening your neck, taking your head forwards and up.

- Try taking the back of your neck up and back for the duration of one of the horse's footfalls.

- Imagine putting more tone into your spine for the time it takes for one of the horse's front feet to step forwards.

- Really lengthen your legs by releasing the hip, softening the ankle joint and sliding your knees down the saddle flaps.

- Take a feel on the outside rein just as the horse's outside foreleg leaves the ground. Try the same thing just as the outside hind leaves the ground and see what responses you get.

- If the bend of the horse is not really well established, make a feel in both reins just when the outside foreleg goes forwards, this will check and rebalance the horse without losing what bend you have.

- If the half-halts are not working, do a row of full halts so that you retune the horse to the aids. Once the halts are working well, reintroduce the half-halt.

- Theoretically every rein aid should be preceded by a leg aid, but if your legs are already in gentle constant contact or if he is ploughing forwards too much it may not be necessary to give an active aid with your legs.

- Make sure you pay attention to the horse's response: if you don't get a response from the half-halt then it didn't work! And you have to be honest with yourself about it not working and repeat the request, perhaps more clearly or in a different way, so that the horse is able to respond.

above If the half-halt is not working, go back to making some full halts.

Jenny asking her four-year-old mare Polly to rebalance her canter with a half-halt as she leaves the fence and heads out across the arena.

In-hand Work 2

...Lightness between the horse and the person has to be built in on the ground and experienced there before they ride him...
– Leslie Desmond

By now the horse should have become quite supple and already understand a lot of what we are asking him to do: he should be accepting a light contact and accepting the touch of the stick on his body; he should also be yielding with his hindquarters and giving us a nice bend both sides etc. Now we can begin to use the art of in-hand work to really practise some gymnastics and yoga with him.

Working in-hand at this stage has a number of benefits: you can see exactly what he is doing and how accurately he is performing the steps, you know the rider is not messing it up because there is no rider, and the horse can try things without the extra weight and balance issues of the rider. The horse also has the advantage of the trainer's body language and direction on the ground beside him, which can better help him to understand what is being asked.

>> **In-hand work is an art in itself** and you need to remind yourself not to expect too much of yourself or the horse in the initial stages. It is going to take patience and practice to get good at it, just like everything else, so stay calm and quiet.

In-hand shoulder-in

The shoulder-in practised in hand is a great way to loosen up your horse, get him thinking about you, put him in the zone and prepared to be ridden.

1. Stand beside the horse's neck/shoulder, so that your stomach is pointing across his chest. Allow enough distance between you and the fence for the horse to make the shoulder-in movement between you and the fence.

2. Beginning on the left rein, hold the inside rein just a couple of inches from the bit with your left hand. Hold the outside rein and stick in your right hand, with the outside rein coming up over the horse's withers and down to your hand at a level just below the saddle flap. You use this outside rein to control the bend and the speed.

3. Ask for a little bend of his head towards you with the inside rein. By bringing both hands towards the centre of the arena a little (away from the fence) you can easily bring the horse's shoulders in away from the fence and you have him in the correct position to do the movement.

4. Have the stick parallel to the ground close to the horse's side, so you can touch him gently behind the girth or on the hindquarters. If he is afraid of the stick you need to teach him the stick is a friendly thing before you can proceed with this level of work.

5. Begin walking with the horse very slowly, feeling the soft bend and relaxation of the jaw with your left fingers. Support him a little with the right rein.

6. Follow and support the forward and sideways movement with the stick if necessary. Make sure the stick is under your control.

7. If he rushes, relax and step more steadily with your feet as you walk.

Caitlin asking for a few steps of four-track shoulder-in from Quarme.

In-hand travers

When shoulder-in has the horse well suppled over a period of training, perhaps days perhaps months, he should be supple and compliant enough to begin making the half-pass movements, which will take his training to a whole new level.

It is often easier to introduce the half-pass movements – travers (haunches-in), renvers (haunches-out) and half-pass – to the horse by starting in the walk in travers, because you have the wall or fence to help you.

1. Walk along the track, placing yourself between the horse and the wall.

2. Hold the rein nearest to you close to the bit as you did for shoulder-in and the opposite rein coming over the neck into your other hand, which also holds the stick, just as with the shoulder-in.

3. Once the horse is walking steadily and coming into a nice shape, use both reins to ask him to bend his head away from you.

4. Place the stick on the hindquarters to ask him to move over and, at the same time, it can help to orient both hands a little towards your body

and away from the horse (that is, in the opposite direction to the way the horse is going). Although that rein aid may seem odd, it works.

In-hand half-pass

Once the horse understands the travers along the wall or fence and can perform it well both ways he is ready to do half-pass. Imagine performing travers along an invisible fence that runs diagonally across the arena, e.g. from the centre line (letter A) to the fence (letter B or E).

In-hand walk pirouette

You can think of the walk pirouette as a very tiny circle in half pass. If the horse understands the half-pass quite well it is a reasonably easy next step to ask for the pirouette by walking yourself around the front end of the horse whilst he is already making half-pass. Make sure he is not too bent in the head or neck to make the pirouette, otherwise he will get stuck or not be able to step around his haunches. Keep the stick along his flank to encourage the outside hind leg to step through rather than falling out of the turn.

The author performing half-pass with Fantastique, looking at her feet and checking she is stepping correctly in accordance with the movement.

The Shoulder-in

If a horse cannot do shoulder-in, it can basically not do anything. Without this exercise the rider has no chance of being able to straighten it (the horse)...

– Anja Beran

The shoulder-in is so amazing it deserves a whole section on its own.

In the shoulder-in the horse moves forwards and sideways, bent through his neck and ribs away from the direction of travel, with his feet making three (or four) tracks when viewed from behind.

The benefits of shoulder-in

Perhaps more than any other movement the shoulder-in helps the horse to become a supple and strong riding horse. It gives the rider a fabulous way of working with each part of the horse and helps the horse to become more symmetrical in the use of his body and hindquarters. Practising the shoulder-in on a regular basis can literally transform a riding horse.

- The shoulder-in helps to engage the hind legs and collect the horse in a very beneficial way.

- The shoulder-in gives you the chance to steer the whole horse accurately without 'losing' one of his shoulders.

- The shoulder-in can be used to help the horse become more flexible and release stiffness in the joints of his hind legs.

- I have seen very one-sided and quite 'cronky' horses go sound and be able to move evenly using shoulder-in.

- The shoulder-in done in walk and trot can help enormously with the quality of the canter.

Nineteen-year-old Fantastique in shoulder-in at the trot with the author. Continued practice of these types of movements can help horses stay sound and supple well into later in life.

>> **Always prepare yourself and the horse** for shoulder-in: make sure you picture the movement in your mind in advance; make sure the horse is listening and he is in the right steady tempo with a correct bend and outline; ask for the movement and then let it happen.

How to do shoulder-in

There are a number of ways to introduce the shoulder-in under saddle. (It should be easier to explain shoulder-in to the horse if you have already practised the movement successfully in-hand). I usually begin to teach the movement in a steady walk and in the initial stages I often ask for counter shoulder-in, which is when the horse's shoulders are taken towards the outside of the arena rather than to the inside (the presence of the fence or wall assist both horse and rider in establishing an understanding of the movement). This gives the horse and rider time to find the right responses and balance. Here are some ways to introduce the shoulder-in.

- In general, both reins should be oriented towards the inside of the bend. The inside rein can be slightly open away from the neck to invite the bend with a light feel, and the outside rein lies quietly against the neck to support the outside shoulder and control the amount of bend in the horse's neck. The rider's shoulders and head should be in agreement with the horse and face in the same direction as the horse's head and shoulders. The rider's inside leg is on the girth as part of the request to bend, the outside leg is a little behind the girth.

- For the best results and for the shoulder-in to be ridden correctly, it should be initiated with the *outside rein*, and not the inside rein. Increasing the feel in the outside rein brings the outside shoulder of the horse in, which is what we want. Using the inside rein (a very common mistake) just brings the horse's nose in, which is not what we want.

- Some horses learn the shoulder-in more easily in the beginning by first making the counter shoulder-in. Ride along the wall or fence on the long

Kate asks Tilly for counter shoulder-in (the bend is to the outside of the arena), where the fence acts as a guide for horse and rider.

side, ask the horse to bend a little to the outside, taking his shoulders a little to the wall or fence; turn your shoulders towards the outside, have your outside leg active on the girth, your inside leg behind the girth and passive; now you are doing counter shoulder-in!

- Ride straight along the track with a tiny bend of the horse's head to the inside. Move both hands four to six inches to the inside of the arena (this will bring the horse's shoulders in away from the wall or fence), turn your own shoulders and head towards the inside so you are facing the same direction as the horse's shoulders and head. Your inside leg is on the girth, your outside leg behind the girth and passive; now you are doing shoulder-in!

- Ride a 6m circle at the beginning of the long side of the arena; this will give you the bend and collection you need for the shoulder-in. As you come back around to the track imagine you are going to make another 6m circle, but after the first step into the circle you change your mind, half-halt and ask the horse to move sideways with your inside leg at the girth. Hey presto, shoulder-in!

- Ride with the horse's legs and body straight along the track but with a slight bend in his head and neck to the inside of the arena. Now gradually increase the *feel* in the outside rein whilst maintaining the inside bend; turn yourself towards the inside so you face across the arena at a 30–40 degree angle and be sure your inside leg is helping the horse to continue along the track. Great – another way to introduce the shoulder-in!

- **Perry's Tip** The moment your horse is in the shoulder-in position you may need to make a half-halt to stop him from just following his nose and walking away across the arena. If the bend is very good you can half-halt with just the outside rein; if the bend isn't brilliant it may help to half-halt with both reins, so that the bend isn't lost.

> ≫ **Always look above the horse's ears,** with your head facing in the same direction as the horse's head. Why? Because you align yourself with the movement, agree with the horse and become more like a centaur.

Variations on the shoulder-in

Once the shoulder-in is established you can do lots of different things with it.

- If you want to have the horse more concentrated, rounder or deeper in the bridle try shoulder-in on a big circle instead of on the straight.

- You can do the occasional tiny circle in shoulder-in as you go around the big circle too, which helps to mobilise and free the horse's pelvis.

- Also try counter shoulder-in on the big circle for a different way of flexing him.

- You can do the shoulder-in with a little more forwardness, but be careful not to unbalance him, and you can do shoulder-in with less forwardness and much more collection to see what helps him.

- Once the shoulder-in is established you can test it by doing it along the centre line or the quarter line too.

- You can do shoulder-in with the horse pretty well straight in his head and neck for more impulsion and engagement behind, or you can experiment with making more bend to help him 'let go' a little more.

- You can do transitions in shoulder-in: walk–halt–walk–halt or trot–walk–trot–walk.

Shoulder-in for competition use should always be a three-track movement, i.e. the sideways angle is only enough that the inside hind leg of the horse follows exactly in the track of the outside foreleg. This type of shoulder-in helps the horse maintain a good forward gait required in the competition arena. The shoulder-in can also be ridden on four tracks and, although this may decrease the forwardness, it can help the horse become rounder and suppler in his pelvis.

Carly asks for shoulder-in on the quarter-line; horse and rider concentrating a lot.

Perry's Tip Anytime the shoulder-in isn't working, don't try to fix it, just ride a small circle and start again.

Improving the Gaits

...It don't mean a thing if it ain't got that swing...

– Duke Ellington

Even seemingly untalented horses can move brilliantly in the pasture when their energy is up and they are having high jinks with their equine companions: their trot is floaty and elevated, their walk is proud and elegant and their canter is collected and powerful. They can spin, pirouette and turn on a sixpence or fly like the wind over the terrain, effortlessly leaping and clearing all manner of obstacles. But then we get on them and ride and, well, it just doesn't seem to work quite the same!

This is where our work to improve the horse's gaits plays an important role. What we are aiming for is for the horse to offer us beautifully elastic, expressive and balanced gaits with ease, lightness, toned muscles and maximum contained energy. Does that sound exciting? Good.

How to improve the walk

- To increase the swing in the walk, ease the reins out in front of you a little, relax your legs and take them slightly behind the girth in *very* light contact with the horse, free up your hips and tickle him – tickle-tickle, tickle-tickle – with the stick high up on the side of his haunches.

Jenny obtaining a nice elastic walk from her young mare, Polly.

- To increase collection in the walk, have the reins quite short but the hands and wrists totally soft; sit proudly with very long light legs and the hips wide open at the top of your legs; take your weight back a millimetre, open your chest, ask him to step well from behind – use tiny touches of the stick if you need them – and keep him in absolute lightness in the hands with little vibrations of the fingers.

- Almost ask for halt and then walk, almost halt and then walk on.

- For even more collection and lightness of step in the walk, wish for two or three soft piaffe steps (trot on the spot) and then walk on, wish for soft piaffe again and then walk on.

- After some real gymnastic work in trot or canter, lateral work, flying changes, or whatever you like, come back to the walk, relax the reins and feel how much he swings his hips, as though the gymnastics have unlocked his pelvis and given the walk a whole new level of activity.

How to improve the trot

- Do loads of transitions, walk–trot–walk–trot, with the horse staying light in the hands and round, maintaining exactly the same shape throughout and sit well yourself. Help him by working on a circle and really keeping the inside bend as it should be, and by giving the aids to go and to come back very soft so there is no reaction to the aids, just smooth ever-lighter responses from the horse as his balance gets better and better with each repetition of the transitions.

- Increase and decrease the pace within the trot as often as four times per 20m circle. This may not be easy to do well in the beginning, but with practice it should develop so all you have to do is change the tone of your spine to make the changes – a fraction freer to go forwards, a fraction less free to collect the trot. Make sure you do this with clear transition moments, rather than gradually winding the trot up and then letting it slob back down again.

- Think more up, up, up for elevation.

- Try making a circle in a good forward trot and start asking for a little shoulder-fore (that is a very shallow shoulder-in) with a good bend, ease out your outside rein a little so the horse can take longer steps with his outside foreleg as he goes around the circle.

- Wish for piaffe (trot on the spot) for a few steps at the beginning of the long side to create a really strong desire in the horse to go, and then allow the horse to trot out down the long side, but don't throw away the contact as you allow the forward surge.

- In trot, ride slightly slower than the horse wants to go until he finds his balance at that speed. And then ride slightly faster than the horse wants to go until he finds his balance at *that* speed. And finally settle into something easy and fantastic.

- Ride some smaller circles, spirals and shoulder-in in trot to get more collection. Move on to riding half-pass movements (travers, renvers and half-pass) and shoulder-in movements alternating them when the horse is ready (see Sequencing Lateral Movements for more ideas).

- Make a few transitions from rein-back–trot–rein-back–trot etc. until they are light, rounded and easy. Do this with minimal, magic aids.

- Turn your hips to the inside of a large circle in trot, this should help to engage the horse's inside hip and place his inside hind leg better under his body.

- With some horses it can be good to ride 'long and low' some of the time in trot. Make sure the horse is not just dribbling along with his chin on the floor but is still rounding down into the bit. Feather-light touches of the inside leg and stick on the inside haunch will help him stretch and step even more elastically into the trot movement.

- Experiment with your rising trot: try making it more economical, try making it more expressive, try leaning forwards, try sitting for a millisecond longer in the saddle, try bringing your seat massively forwards instead of up when you rise, try staying standing in the stirrups, try bouncing the heels down-down-down-down each time you rise and each time you sit, try tucking your bum emphatically underneath you for the rise and the sit. All of these variations can expand the horse's trot, and your horse will show you instantly which ones work for him.

Lovely ground-covering trot from Fiona and Relento.

How to improve the canter

- A lot of the work we do with the horse is about creating good habits, and that goes for the good habit of doing a well-balanced canter. To achieve this, do only a few canter strides – just as many as the horse can do without losing his balance and rushing (often only about six strides) – and then come back to walk and start again. Over time he will learn to stay balanced in the canter for longer.

- Keep things calm; don't push him in the canter.

- To make the canter more expressive and collected, take the canter from the walk, or the shoulder-in in the walk, or even the rein-back or the piaffe.

- Canter with your legs and body but every few strides, *think* for just a moment of coming to the walk with your reins and head, but stay in canter, this will collect and round the canter, placing the horse back onto his haunches more.

- Release and relax your inside leg well down and forwards in the canter to see if its helps the horse.

- Try reducing the size of some of the circles in the canter to collect the hindquarters. You could ride a spiral, reducing the circles as you go in, then spiral him back out onto the big circle to start your inward spiral again.

- If the horse falls out of canter it is usually because he lost his balance, it is therefore pointless to rush him back into canter as though he's being a naughty boy. Instead regroup, slow down and start the canter again; that way you get the bonus of another gymnasticising transition up into canter. Perfect!

- For more activity in the canter take a little bit of counter-canter then go back to true canter. Counter-canter is the horse cantering 'on the wrong leg', that means going round the right cantering on the left lead and vice versa.

- If the canter is too flat or inexpressive make sure you keep your outside leg behind the girth for the duration of the canter. This will also help the horse to stay in the canter.

- Imagine the canter being slow, like the speed of a steady trot, and imagine the feeling of the canter happening underneath you, not rushing out the front of you. Now imagine the canter being at the speed of the walk.

- Look past the horse's outside ear in canter – it will help both of you.

- Lungeing the horse with correctly adjusted side-reins in canter can really help him to find his balance and rhythm before he is burdened with the extra challenge of the weight of the rider.

- If the canter is difficult, forget it for a few days, weeks or months and work on the quality of the horse's work in the walk and trot. When he does brilliant half-pass in trot he will probably do great canters without you even working at it.

Advanced Lateral Work

The Classical principles of riding recommend lateral
movements as a basic exercise. Many riders reject this as
such exercises are thought to ruin the horse's joints. The
opposite is the case!

– Dr Gerd Heuschmann

Having developed the shoulder-in over a period of weeks or months the horse will have become nicely supple and responsive in his lateral work. Now he is ready for the next level: introducing the half-pass movements. These movements – travers (haunches-in), renvers (haunches-out) and half-pass – are the pinnacle of lateral exercises. They are more demanding and add to the level of collection and athleticism in the horse, they also increase the level of sophistication in the way the horse and rider connect and communicate with one-another.

In the half-pass, the horse moves forwards and sideways bent *towards* the direction of movement. This is the opposite of all the lateral movements attempted so far. It is possible to do these lateral movements in all three basic gaits: walk, trot and canter, and for the really advanced horse in the passage (highly elevated trot) too. I find it is often most beneficial to begin teaching these movements in quite a slow and collected walk.

Travers

The horse travels along the fence or wall, bent in the direction of travel, with his haunches in towards the inside of the arena.

Renvers

The horse travels along the fence or wall, bent in the direction of travel, with his haunches out against the fence, and with his shoulders/forehand towards the inside of the arena.

Ginger, Jenny's thirteen-year-old TB x ID eventer in travers at the canter.

A very nice example of renvers from Fiona and Relento.

Half-pass

The horse travels forwards and sideways across the middle of the arena, bent in the direction of travel, with his shoulders leading slightly ahead of his haunches.

>> **The feel of the half-pass** often surprises people because it doesn't feel quite as 'sideways' as they expect; this is because the shoulders of the horse go ahead of the haunches, rather than the whole horse moving sideways 'in one piece'.

How to do the half-pass movements

- With these movements, when we say 'inside' what we mean here is on the concave side of the bend. So if we are bending the horse around the right leg and making a half-pass, he has a right bend and the 'inside' is on the right.

The half-pass is a graceful movement, as well as being very useful for suppling the horse.

- The best position for the hands in the half-pass movements is to have the inside rein placed close to the horse's neck, asking for the bend but with a soft, passive feel, and the outside rein can be opened away from the neck to help maintain the sideways position of the horse, but must not be pulled backwards to conflict with the bend. (These hand positions will be pretty much the opposite of their positions for movements attempted so far).

- The inside leg is forwards and active at the girth, with the horse bending around this leg. The outside leg is behind the girth, supporting the idea of going sideways, but fairly quiet and light. (If the outside leg is too active or strong it will push the horse's ribs the wrong way and change the horse's bend).

- The easiest place to introduce the half-pass movements to the horse is the long side of the school. Riding straight along the track, keep your inside leg well forward, ease the outside leg behind the girth, have the inside rein against the neck and open the outside rein away from the neck. The horse will now be bent around your inside leg with his head still facing straight down the track; his haunches will have come towards the inside of the arena by a few inches so that he is moving laterally. This movement is the travers (haunches in).

- Make sure you always turn your head and shoulders to be in absolute alignment with the angle of the movement.

- A way to ask for a few first steps of half-pass is to ride along the quarter-line (5m from the fence) in shoulder-in, so that the horse is bent towards the fence. In this position he is in the ideal bend and angle for the half-pass, so all you need do is relax the inside leg forwards and down a little, relax the rein that is asking for the bend a little (whilst still maintaining the bend), open the other rein a few inches from the horse's neck (even though it seems totally weird), place a little of your weight in the direction of the half-pass movement and give a single nudge behind the girth with your so-called outside leg to ask the horse to step forwards and sideways towards the fence.

- Try achieving half-pass this way: begin to ride a diagonal line from the centre line at letter C or letter A towards B or E. Whilst both you and the horse maintain your gaze on the destination letter (B or E), slide your legs and reins into their half-pass positions: the rein that will be on the inside of the bend stays close to the neck and the leg on that side goes forwards and down for the horse to bend around; the rein on the outside of the bend opens away from the neck and the leg on the outside of the bend goes well behind the girth to suggest to him the idea of his haunches going sideways.

- Try starting to ask for travers prior to the corner *before* you get to the long-side on which you want the movement. That way the horse's rear end is already away from the fence at the correct position and so is your seat. Basically you never allow the haunches to reach the fence, which means you don't have to try getting them off the fence again to ride the travers!

- Try starting in the counter shoulder-in, with the horse going sideways along the fence bent away from the direction of movement. When he is going calmly and well, smoothly change the bend so that it becomes travers.

- Always stay relaxed in your body, legs and hands and keep the aids very light whilst asking for these movements, otherwise you make it harder or impossible for the horse.

- The horse can start to use travers as an evasion; as a way to avoid going straight along the fence. This is especially true in canter, where his natural crookedness colludes with the position for the travers. Make sure you only use travers to teach the horse the spirit of the movement and afterwards only sparingly. The half-pass and renvers have less evasion potential, so ultimately use those movements more than travers.

- If the half-pass lacks angle or clarity, instead of booting the horse sideways more with the outside leg, simply open the outside rein about a foot from the horse's neck for a stride or two. This will re-align the horse's haunches and make him step more sideways behind; strange but true!

Sequencing Lateral Movements

Dressage for the horse; not the horse for dressage.

– Bent Branderup

Once you have a few different lateral movements in your horse's repertoire you can start to use them for increased effect by juxtaposing them with one another, e.g. ride shoulder-in and then flow into travers. By sequencing the lateral movements in this way you can help the horse to use himself in different ways and different parts of his frame, increasing his strength and suppleness to a new level. This work also means he becomes more fluid in his responses and in his movement and *really* listens to you. Of course the movements need to be ridden accurately so that you don't just find yourself doodling around all over the place going sideways. Decide on a plan and follow it, and then see what results it gives you in the responses of the horse: by this stage you should be able to do that quite well.

Some ideas for sequences

- Ride shoulder-in on the long side, ride the short side normally and then counter shoulder-in on the next long side.

- Ride shoulder-in on one long side and then travers on the next long side.

- Alternate shoulder-in and travers (it means you keep the same bend but just turn yourself and the horse) on the same long side.

- Alternate shoulder-in and renvers on the same long side (the angle of the horse stays the same, but the bend has to change whilst he is on the move.

- Ride a 20m circle, begin in shoulder-in and then go to travers on the same circle (that means the bend stays the same) and then go back to the shoulder-in to finish.

- Ride shoulder-in on a 20m circle, and then counter shoulder-in on the same circle (you have to change the bend as you turn him to face the outside of the circle for counter shoulder-in).

- Ride half-pass for a few steps, shoulder-in for a few steps and half-pass for a few steps (this means keeping the bend and angle the same, just changing the direction he is heading with his feet.

- Ride leg-yield to the long side and then immediately shoulder-in (this keeps the same bend).

Shoulder-in on the centre line. Here it is being used to prepare the horse to flow into half-pass; notice the bend and angle of the horse are already in place to go into half-pass.

The horse, prepared with a few steps of shoulder-in, is now taken across the arena in half-pass.

- Ride half-pass from the quarter line to the long side then counter shoulder-in to keep the bend, or shoulder-in, which requires him to change the bend.

- Ride half-pass to the long side and then go into renvers (keep the bend, taking care to make the change to renvers delicately).

- In walk or canter, whilst in the half-pass you could ride a tiny semi-circle and then half-pass back to where you started from; this will be a half-pirouette. One day it could become a whole tiny circle in half-pass – a full pirouette in walk or canter!

By now you will have developed quite a feel for what the horse is doing and what he needs next, and so you can start to structure your own plans for sequences of lateral movements that specifically address the areas your horse needs help with. Enjoy.

The Piaffe

...As a result of the appropriate gymnastics and training of the horse, the appearance and the movements of the horse will be more beautiful...

– Colonel Alois Podhajsky

The piaffe is the most collected form of trot, where the horse trots but covers almost no ground in front. He should do this in rounded self-carriage, in an even rhythm and with his haunches lowered. Whilst the piaffe done with perfection is a highly advanced movement, I am including it here because, even by making a couple of half-steps in the piaffe (something attainable by most horses), the rider has at their fingertips a fantastically useful tool for gymnasticising the horse and helping in so many ways.

The benefits of piaffe

- The horse learns to really collect himself, with a shortened frame and lowered haunches.

- The horse learns not to just push forwards into the bridle.

- Piaffe is a good way to build impulsion before asking for a bigger trot.

- It is a great way to collect the horse before a transition to canter, helping the canter itself to become much more rounded, collected and balanced.

- It makes the horse like a coiled spring, ready for just about anything.

- It really strengthens the horse's hindquarters, supples the joints of his hind legs and increases his carrying power.

The most collected form of trot, the piaffe is proof of the horse's willingness and lightness to the aids, both to go forwards and to remain in place at the same time.

How to prepare for the piaffe

Making a correct piaffe is the final result of long-term work with the horse, helping him to become refined to the aids, strong, supple and calmly obedient. Here are some of the things you can do to work towards preparing for the piaffe and, as you can see, they are not rocket-science and are all quite doable.

1. The horse needs to be amazingly responsive to light touches of your legs.

2. The horse needs to stay well rounded (on the bit) in his work, especially transitions.

3. The horse needs to be brilliant at transitions between walk, trot, halt and rein-back in any combination.

4. The horse needs to be trained to stay beautifully straight, which is mostly achieved by the shoulder-in.

5. The horse needs to be wonderfully polite and light in the contact.

Ten tips for asking for piaffe

1. Make sure you look up and forwards (looking down or at the horse is likely to confuse him into not moving, going backwards or even rearing).

2. Although it makes theoretical sense to ask for piaffe from trot (because it is the same rhythm), the forward urge and balance of trotting can make it difficult to achieve in that fashion. To start with it may be easier to ask for piaffe from a very collected walk.

3. It can be useful in the beginning to allow the horse to move forwards a little with each step in the piaffe, only looking for the perfection of trotting on the spot after much training.

4. Place your lower legs quite a long way back (a similar position to that for the rein-back usually works); this position stimulates lots of impulsion, lowers the haunches and helps to limit the horse's forward stride.

5. Keep the hands and contact very light, with the horse nicely rounded and collected. Help him to stay totally light in the bridle with little vibrations of the fingers of the hand on whichever side of his jaw you feel him tightening.

6. Help the horse to stay straight; oddly, you can do that by keeping him in a slight shoulder-in position.

7. Avoid any strong aids – we want to give the horse the idea of piaffe, and thence *invite* him to do it. Strong legs are apt to make him shoot forwards or stop moving his back feet altogether. Strong reins will create resistance or stop him from moving his front feet.

8. Think of light trot, feel his back moving in a soft trot movement, stimulate his hind legs to trot with little touches of your calves.

9. Touch exceedingly lightly with the stick or have an assistant on the ground doing that job, finding the horse's tickly spot that encourages activity.

10. When the horse makes a couple of little steps, stop and reward.

How to introduce the piaffe

- Try making lots of calm, quality and energetic transitions between trot and rein-back. Make four or five steps backwards and then five or six steps in trot. When the horse gets really smart at the exercise reduce the number of trot and rein-back steps. Once he starts anticipating the trot you have the chance to ask him to pause and allow a couple of piaffe steps.

- When he is nicely round in walk and wanting to trot, slide your legs back and very lightly breathe on him with your calves, wishing for a couple of steps of piaffe instead of trotting. If he does it, forget the trot, drop the reins and let him know what a great idea he just had.

- Ride a shallow shoulder-in and alternate between three or four steps of walk and three or four of trot all down the long side of the arena. At some point he will be in shallow shoulder-in in walk anticipating trotting, and you can again ask him to pause in that position and make a couple of piaffe steps.

- When riding out, if his friends trot or gallop away and his energy comes up, keep him straight, use your intention and the core of your body, rather than pulling the reins, and keep him where he is as you ask for a few steps of piaffe.

Flying Changes

*...As a rule, the horse must take pleasure in his work. Otherwise,
he and his rider will not be able to accomplish anything graceful...*
– Antoine de Pluvinel

The flying change is when the horse changes from one canter lead to the other whilst staying in canter. Some horses find this movement easier than other horses; some horses find it a lot easier from one lead to another. The tricky thing about flying changes is that you either get one or you don't, which means you can only really work on achieving flying changes successfully by working on the preparation for the change.

How to prepare for flying changes

For flying changes you need the following ingredients.

1. A well-balanced, bounding canter with good impulsion and elevation.

2. The ability to canter forwards and sideways (canter half-pass)

3. Instantaneous walk-to-canter strike-offs, 100 per cent accurately on the correct lead every time with no delay after asking for the canter, i.e. there must be an *instant* canter response from the horse.

American author and ecuyer Paul Belasik mid-flying change. This picture is useful to look at, because you really can see that fraction of a second when the horse is switching hind legs as he changes from left canter lead to right canter lead.

4. Some ability in counter-canter, although too much ease in the counter-canter can make it difficult to train the horse to make the flying change.

5. The rider needs to know the feeling and timing of flying changes on a physical level (I recommend students go and ride many many changes on schoolmaster horses to acquire familiarity with the feeling of the movement).

6. It is important to understand that the flying change starts behind you with the horse's hindquarters before it reaches his front legs. It also helps to understand which is your horse's best canter lead, as he will probably make the flying change more easily from his strong canter lead to his weak one.

> **Make sure you and the horse stay calm** when working towards changes. Keep your aids very quiet, otherwise he may burst forwards and go a little crazy. Avoid swinging the horse's head around or messing with the bend too much when asking for a flying change – the more you mess with the front end the greater your chance of mistakenly making the horse change in front and not behind.

How to introduce the flying change

There are a variety of ways of introducing the flying change. It can help to try different ways to introduce the idea of flying changes to different horses, hopefully finding a way that your horse understands best. After he gets the idea of changing you can refine it and ask for the movement in different parts of the arena. Here are some suggestions for how to try for the first changes.

- Ride half-pass in canter from the quarter line to the track, arriving at the track at the end of the long side, just before the corner. As the corner approaches ask for the change by switching your leg position and giving a 'pop' with the new outside leg well behind the girth.

- Ask for a very small circle in canter, not quite a pirouette, but certainly a circle that puts the horse on his haunches. You may feel him want to shift his weight out of the circle, at which point switch the position of your legs from true canter to the other lead and allow him to escape from the small circle by changing direction; he will make a flying change and canter away.

- Ride around the short side of the arena in canter and at the beginning of the long side ask for two or three walk steps, during which you change the bend to renvers; and then ask for counter-counter down the long side. Do the same pattern a few times until he anticipates the renvers and counter-canter, then do exactly the same exercise in the same place without coming back to walk, which means you should get a flying change.

- Many riders try asking for a change at the centre line (letter X) when crossing the arena; this often results in the horse changing in front first, which we want to avoid, but if you are intent on trying it that way, start by tackling it like this: as you approach the centre line use your outside leg behind the girth to bend him and move his haunches over a little (think of creating a little tension in his body). As you approach the change point count down to yourself '3-2-1-change' and release the horse from the tension by bringing the outside leg forwards, allowing him to choose to perform a flying change.

- In counter-canter at the beginning of the long side ask for three or four steps of leg-yield towards the quarter line, then ask for half-pass back to the wall; as the horse reaches the wall he may well be ready to change.

- In true canter at the beginning of the long side ask for three or four steps of half-pass towards the quarter line; keep the bend the same and ask for leg-yield back to the wall. Some horses choose to change at the point of being asked for the leg-yield.

> **》 Timing is everything when asking for changes.** Every horse has his own response time, but in general if you count to yourself '3–2–1–change' and give the actual aid by switching your legs from one canter lead to the other in the gap between the '1' and the 'change' you will give the horse time to respond in the right moment.

Golden Nuggets –
Quotes from Perry's Clinics

- Be the walk, trot and canter with your whole being, with everything you've got. Be the rhythm with your whole body. Have total commitment with everything you do with the horse.

- Sometimes you really have to keep the outside rein: it appears to defy logic, but it works.

- What was your thought just before what happened happened?

- Let your knees float next to the saddle and see what happens.

- Look ahead – see the horse with your peripheral vision.

- We have a wonderful experience and we expect it to feel as good the next day, but even if it is the same, we won't feel the same because it's no longer new, so just follow the path that took you to the original experience, that's all.

- Let the weight of your legs hang.

- Big changes need time to become familiar.

- A young horse needs lots of simple riding so it has a safe place to come back to.

- Open yourself to the forward motion – be willing to go with your whole body.

- It's incredible what kind of conversations you can have with the horse when your hands are quiet.

- Anything can happen at any moment. We can't afford to drift off. Horses love it when we are present, because they are present all of the time – never in the past or future.

- The action of the rein goes through the horse's body and connects with his hind feet.

- Be observant, not judgmental. Examine: how did that happen? What did I do? Then you can really learn.

- Be smooth in all your movements.

- Sit on your 'Rumpa!'

- 'Horse-whispering', not 'horse-wrestling'! Use your tact and intelligence to deal with problems, rather than getting in a fight with the horse; horses are easily upset and a lot bigger and stronger than we are. Getting in a fight with the horse breaks the trust between you, and runs the risk of him finding out how puny you really are.

- Horses really like it when we know what we are doing.

- I find it exciting that so much that can happen internally in us influences such a big creature (the horse).

- Horses know our thoughts and intentions, so they must be the first aids.

- It's the quality of your spine that can so influence the horse.

- It will never be a partnership of equals – the horse is superior to us in so many ways, that's why we have to take the leadership role, otherwise we're sunk!

- We need to be cantering the whole time we want the horse to canter. If we aren't cantering, the horse can't.

- When the horse starts to get emotionally unsettled it's even more important to show him that actually all that's required is: 'just this'.

- Passively be there, asking the horse.

- Allow with the body to ask the horse to go forwards and support with the leg and stick.

- If we notice when we are doing things right, it's easy to build on that and make progress – to say 'yes I'll do more of that'. We can learn more easily that way.

- It can be an amazing conversation to-ing and fro-ing between you and the horse.

- If the fruit isn't ripe, leave it on the tree.

- Pick up or shorten the reins without tensing or compromising the rest of you.

- Breathe more life force into you so that the movement has more ease.

- Ask yourself 'what can I change to get what I want?'

- The optimum balance point in the saddle is making use of gravity – don't argue with the planet!

- You don't have to keep stopping and patting him all the time, just send him love with your heart and soul whilst still working – he'll hear it and know he's doing well.

For more quotes from Perry's clinics visit **www.perry-wood.com**, or visit a clinic

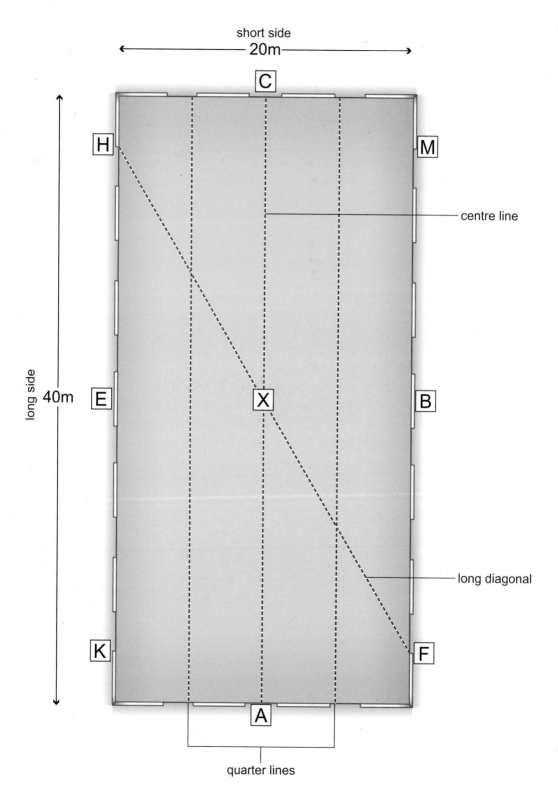

short side
20m

long side
40m

centre line

long diagonal

quarter lines